Bought

God's direction for spending, saving, giving, investing and getting out of debt

Study what the Bible has to say about how we handle money and possessions and gain fresh insights for your walk of faith

Mark Lloydbottom

Copyright @2016 by Your Money Counts

All rights reserved.

Published by Your Money Counts, UK.

Unless otherwise noted, Scripture quotations are from the Holy Bible:

The Holy Bible, New International Version®, NIV® Copyright © 1973, 1978, 1984, 2011 by Biblica, Inc.® Used by permission. All rights reserved worldwide.

Verses identified as NASB are taken from the New American Standard Bible, Copyright © 1960, 1962, 1963, 1968, 1971, 1972, 1973, 1975, 1977, 1995 by the Lockman Foundation.

Verses identified as NKJV are taken from the New King James Version, Copyright © 1982 by Thomas Nelson, Inc.

Verses identified as NLT are taken from the Holy Bible: New Living Translation, Copyright © 1996, 2004 by Tyndale Charitable Trust. Used by permission of Tyndale House Publishers.

Verses identified as AMP are taken from the Amplified Bible, Copyright © 1954, 1958, 1962, 1964, 1965, 1987 by the Lockman Foundation.

Verses identified as KJV are taken from the King James Version of the Bible: Public Domain.

Verses identified as TLB are taken from The Living Bible, Copyright © 1973 by the Zondervan Corporation.

ISBN: 978-1-908423-14-6

Printed in the United Kingdom

Design: Dickie Dwyer

Layout: Loulita Gill

With thanks

My thanks are due to Howard Dayton who was the original author of **Your Money Counts** which was first published in the United States. Without his commitment to developing studies to highlight the importance that God attaches to the handling of money and possessions **Bought** would not have seen the light of day. I am particularly grateful to Howard for the many hours he allowed me to spend with him drawing from his experience and understanding of God's Word regarding how we can better manage our money and possessions from a biblical perspective.

My thanks also to all those who have helped me publish this new version. I am particularly grateful to Gillian Searl for her editing expertise, Peter Briscoe, the European director of Compass with whom we are affiliated. Philip Bishop and Dickie Dwyer have been of immense help in the update of this book and to them I am thankful for their expertise and persistence.

I am also grateful to Crown Financial Ministries in the United States as they first gave permission for us to publish Howard's book in the United Kingdom. And finally, my wife Rhoda deserves my special thanks for joining me on life's journey and helping keep our finances in order God's way.

Mark Lloydbottom

Your Money Counts
www.yourmoneycounts.org.uk

"All Scripture is God-breathed and is useful for teaching, rebuking, correcting and training in righteousness, so that the man of God may be thoroughly equipped for every good work."

2 Timothy 3:16

Foreword

Navigating our way through life can be hard. With little money education in our schools, and many families not talking about money much, it can be left to us to find our own way through the money maze. This book provides a map to navigate that maze, blending biblical insight with common sense from Mark Lloydbottom's life experience. Sound Christian thinking on money frees us from misconceptions about where our security lies, about what we need rather than want, and helps us adopt alternative values and priorities in life – ones which set us free from the pressures that money can bring.

However good we are with managing our money, whether we're comfortably off or struggling to get by, our position is no different – we're stewards – looking after that which is entrusted to us by a generous God. Stewardship is not just about giving – it's far wider than that. Stewardship encompasses buying, saving, investing and giving decisions.

Even after many years of seeking to adopt a Christian framework for living out my life, my stewardship of money and possessions is still a matter I need to engage with frequently and I've found this book to be a helpful challenge to my thinking. It has made me simultaneously thankful for all that I've received and renewed my commitment to wise biblical stewardship.

Dr John Preston
National Stewardship Officer, Church of England

Table of contents

PART 1

9   An introduction: Issues and problems

11   My story

22   Financial insights

34   The problem

PART 2

45   The Bible: a blueprint for living

47   Ownership

52   Stewardship

PART 3

61 Free to serve Him

63 Debt

78 Getting out of debt

95 Counsel - seeking Godly wisdom

PART 4

107 Growing in generosity

109 Giving

125 Tithing

PART 5

133 Save. Invest. Spend.

135 Saving and investing

151 Spending

165 Standard of living

174 Perspectives

PART 6

187 Summing it all up

189 Do you feel like you are in a crisis?

An introduction: Issues and problems

My story | Financial insights | The problem

The handling of money is one aspect of life that most of us think about every day. Some have enough to satisfy their wants. Others never seem to have enough – sometimes there is too much month at the end of the money!

Some struggle to work out how much money is enough.

Newspapers...media...social media...the internet. There is no shortage of those wishing to impart their wisdom.

The Bible also has a lot to say about money and possessions, and for Christians that has to be a great place to start seeking guidance and good counsel.

PART 1 | CHAPTER 1

My story

FROM CHILD TO ADULT; FROM MISTAKES TO MISSION

I returned home after playing football at school – I was drenched from the downpour a few minutes earlier as I squelched up to the front door. I had scored a couple of good goals, but missed some sitters. My shoes were soaked and scuffed and I knew that my mother would have something to say as they were less than a week old. I rang the doorbell to our flat, but there was no reply. That meant mum was late returning from work, and with my brother staying on at chess club I knew I would be alone for some time. I found the key hidden under the stone by the dustbin and let myself in as I always did twice a week. I was destined never to forget that day.

As I entered our living room I looked at the television and wondered if it was time to watch Andy Pandy – a programme that always seemed entertaining but by today's standards definitely even beyond old fashioned. After Andy Pandy I would watch Blue Peter with Christopher Trace and Lelia Williams. With ten minutes before it was time to switch on the black and white Bush television I sat and stared around the room. My eyes were attracted to a pile of papers and I got up with my wet socks still hugging my feet and approached the table with a measure of curiosity. I looked and wanted to take a peek – my first recollection of being nosey.

Mum's weekly letter from gran, a form from the Inland Revenue (now referred to as HMRC), a few of her exquisitely handwritten notes and then I saw a bank statement. What was this I wondered? I recall seeing mum along with others go into 'my bank' and I had begun to work out some aspects of how our home finances worked, but this was the first bank statement I had ever seen. I looked intensely; debit, credit – what did those words mean? In the credit column there was an entry that had my dad's initials alongside. I had never really known any parent other than my mum; others had a dad at home, but not me and my brother. I later discovered that they had separated five years earlier. My eyes were drawn toward the final column. This was headed 'balance' and even as a seven year old that was a word I instinctively comprehended.

Thirteen pounds ten shillings – is that all we have left to live on? I was gripped with worry as I asked myself 'how are we going to survive?'

Suddenly, I heard the key turning in the lock and realised that mum was home so I hurriedly collected the papers and replaced them how I had found them a few moments earlier. I raced over to the television and turned the set on – by the time mum came in the screen was 'warming up' and the familiar signature tune of Blue Peter could be heard as the sea and ship became clearer on the ever glowing screen. What about Andy Pandy I thought? I realised how long I had been looking at the bank statement, what I thought it showed and what I perceived was our perilous financial situation. I had little interest in Christopher Trace's models, not even the ones he had made earlier, for all I could think about was my discovery that mum had little or no money and we were in trouble.

EARLY LEARNING

Thus my childhood was partly framed by knowing there was no money other than for basics. How did finance flow into the household? Well, I worked out that it only trickled and came from mum's job as a receptionist at a dental practice, my absent father and gifts from my uncle. The home finances did not allow for anything other than the basics of food, clothes and rent. Clothing? I always looked forward to mum taking me shopping for clothes. The 'Nearly New' shop in Wolverhampton supplied our household with just about everything we required. Eating out? Occasionally, mum would take me out to one of two Chinese restaurants that had recently opened, although those outings ceased when the local newspaper reported that one of those restaurants was accused of killing cats and serving them as chicken.

No matter how challenging mum found her finances, I later realised how careful she had been as a manager of our home finances. Her stewardship enabled us to move from the flat she rented to a house. She told me she now had a mortgage, a term I did not understand.

Like any youngster I wanted to be able to spend – sweets and superman comics were top of my list. At the age of eight I joined the local church choir where, provided I attended practice on Fridays and both Sunday services, I could earn nine (old) pence. We were paid quarterly and so I looked forward to the choir master giving me my brown envelope containing almost ten shillings (50p). Whenever I sang at a wedding I earned 2/6d (12.5p) and sometimes there were three weddings on a Saturday, so that was a day to look forward to, especially as the pay was handed out at the end of the wedding service, almost as soon as the last guest had left to join the photo call.

TIME FOR WORK

My first interview was with Chubb, whose business had started in Wolverhampton in 1820 and is now a global enterprise. I was 17 and had never before been interviewed. My next interview was with an insurance company: "What is the purpose of insurance?" I could not answer, but I do recall being told that the right answer was 'using the money of the fortunate to help those who are not so fortunate.' Next I sat opposite a bank manager. I noticed his well furnished office, and as he sat behind his large desk with a broad smile I looked up and tried to be as composed as I could. I was accustomed to teachers, been afraid of the headmaster and deputy head, but was not used to being interviewed for a job. Mum suggested I give my father a call. So I called dad and told him about my interview experiences and he told me that with the jobs I had applied for I would be waiting for 'dead men's shoes.' Three interviews and no job offer – I was on a steep learning curve and in need of an employer.

I returned to the Youth Employment Bureau, the office which back in the sixties was charged with providing assistance to help school leavers take their first steps into the job market. I recounted my experiences to Mr Mills, the chief Youth Employment Officer, and after completing some tests was advised to go and have an interview with an accountant. My brother was an articled clerk and studying to be a chartered accountant and so I knew that this required a lot of studying, but at the end of the rainbow I would be able to earn abundantly. This interview was different. I was talking to Malcolm Gilbert who was the liaison officer for all accountancy firms in Wolverhampton. He was responsible for interviewing prospective trainees and then reassigning their applications to other firms. "I would like to offer you a job." Those words were music to my ears. I was there, on my way – now I would be able to go to all the Wolves home games and maybe even some away ones, as well as being able to buy some trendy clothes.

TRAINING TO BE AN ACCOUNTANT

I started my training in Wolverhampton, and having passed my first two professional exams in double quick time, I decided to take advantage of an Institute of Chartered Accountants scheme allowing me to take a training break and spend six months working in industry. At the age of 20 I left home and drove my Morris Minor estate to Southampton where I had a room booked at the YMCA and a job in 'fixed assets' at a synthetic rubber company. I knew what fixed assets were, but why would it need a whole department?

Shortly after starting there I was called into the chief accountant's office, "Will you go and work on the production line? Your salary will continue and we will pay you for working on the line." This was the early seventies and strikes were commonplace. The workers at the Hythe plant had gone on strike for more pay while the syndicate of rubber company owners were demanding that production continue. I had doubled my salary during these six months in industry and now it was going to quadruple. On my first day as a manual worker I approached the factory entrance in my car. Ahead of my gleaming bonnet I could see a lot of people milling around the factory gate. As I drew closer I saw police jostling with strikers, whose job I was about to undertake. I slowed down and drove slowly through the turbulent mass of bodies. I was used to being part of a swaying crowd at football, but never one as angry as this. I drove through the picket line accompanied by a cacophony of shouting. I experienced excitement and terror in those scary moments – especially as the local television company was there filming for the evening news reports. I thought how envious some of my friends would be if they knew what I was experiencing – after all they were still auditing! As I parked with the noise echoing in the distance, I looked at my car. I had bought it from a friend who had looked after it with great care for over 70,000 miles, but now there were cigarette burns all down the sides. I realised I had crossed a line that some thought was not mine to traverse and they used their cigarettes to show their disapproval.

That evening I watched the local news and saw the reports from outside the factory gate. Strikes were almost inevitably about more pay and this one was no exception as workers demanded a pay increase of 15%. That evening I reflected; never did I imagine that I would be a 'scab.' Why should I? After all, I had decided to train to become an accountant!

We were all instructed to meet at the company's Southampton offices the next day as arrangements had been made to transfer us to the Hythe plant. As the minibus with its ten occupants approached the gates we could see TV cameras, police and a seething mass of workers. As we slowly passed down the picket line the minibus was rocked from side to side as the strikers let us know they vehemently disapproved of what we were doing. Angry faces were centimetres from the window as they banged on the glass and shouted, 'scab, scab.' I was probably more frightened that day than the previous one. The police were outnumbered and unable to hold back the line of fire that was directed toward those who had dared to accept management's request to 'keep the plant' going.

I headed toward the synthetic rubber production line and the coagulation tanks for another day of watching rubber bales pass by. I reflected about those on the picket line I had just passed through, their commitment to the cause for increased pay and their anger as we had broken through their line. I reflected on how important money was to them as well as to me. I had accepted the opportunity because it seemed like an adventure and a way to make money. I had little time to contemplate further as the foreman, Mr Wood, a towering man also known as 'timber,' entered the canteen to bark out instructions. He was a man I instantly learned to respect and obey; his presence was commanding as he sought to show the white collar staff how to keep the intolan bales moving. I looked at the dark yellow bales and wondered what happened to them after they left the plant – how did they become tyres?

FINDING MY WIFE

At Above Bar Church in Southampton I met Rhoda, a woman to whom I was immediately attracted. She was recently divorced and had a young baby, Philip. We married within a year and settled down. At the end of six months I found a new employer who agreed to continue my training contract. The salary remained low and I struggled to provide my new family with anything but the basics. Now I had a wife and child to provide for, but we had both been used to living on low incomes and so were well prepared. Little did our next door neighbours know that when they offered us food from their garden or their store cupboard we barely had enough for our next meal. Our shopping was supplemented by luncheon vouchers which were given to me as a perk. Tough times? Yes, to us they were, but we were happy and totally in love – little else really mattered.

PREPARING ACCOUNTS IN BRISTOL

After qualifying we moved to Bristol and I found an accountancy firm looking to employ staff who had qualified with a national firm.

"Come and see me please Mark." As I entered the partners' office he greeted me and asked me to take a seat. "At your interview you asked not to prepare any more farm accounts" (I worked on preparing farm accounts in Wolverhampton and found that farmers' records were often smelly and very incomplete). I would like you to go to…. The following Monday I drove to the farm in south Bristol to start work on preparing six years' worth of accounts. I was greeted by the farmer's wife and introduced to the family. Soon I was sitting in an 'office' in the farmhouse loft. I looked around and found post that hadn't been opened for six years – hundreds of unopened envelopes!

I was invited to join the family for lunch. The farmer's wife and son chatted freely while the farmer sat sullenly without uttering one word. This was a new experience for me and it felt a little uncomfortable.

"How do you know which bills to pay?", I asked. It occurred to me during the four hours of opening old unopened post that they must have a different system of paying bills.

"We wait until John, the bailiff comes; he tells us what to pay."

"Oh, that's interesting," I responded. I had found two envelopes with out-of-date cheques.

"What about cheques for the sale of cattle and crops?" I enquired.

"I know what those envelopes look like" was Joan's reply.

As the week passed I progressed with the accounts preparation and lunch times became a little more relaxed as the conversation widened. However the farmer did little more than grunt as he sat at the head of the table looking very morose.

By lunchtime on Friday, I could see the farm was in severe financial straits. As I opened the letters from the bank I could see the manager was concerned at the state of the finances. Over lunch, I mentioned that the farm was in deep financial straits,

"Did they know?," I awkwardly enquired.

The weekend was enjoyable; we went to the park to fly kites and then shopping in the afternoon to buy the suite we had been planning to purchase for six months. We had made friends with a lot of other couples living in our avenue, it was summer and we spent the weekend socialising with our neighbours.

Monday morning and on the journey to the farm I contemplated my plans for completing the accounts. I thought of sandwiches in the pub rather than lunch in the farmhouse. As I turned the corner I was confronted with flashing blue lights and as I looked ahead I could see an ambulance and three police cars. "Come in please, we would like to speak with you." As I passed through the farm I could see the family crying as they were coming to terms with finding the farmer hanging in the barn. The strain of trying to make the farm profitable had taken its toll and he had given up on solving the farm's financial problems.

Six months later the same partner called, "Come in and see me please Mark."

Once I was sat in his office he said, "we have a construction company that is owned by a very astute client, he is an accountant and we need you to go and finalise the company accounts. He has prepared draft accounts which show a profit of £140,000. The bank is asking for audited figures as the cash flow is quite tight."

A week later I reported back to the partner with accounts that showed a loss of £120,000.

"Do you know what you are doing?" The question was asked more than a little tersely.

"Yes", I said "I know the accounts are different from the client's and I can explain why. There is a serious problem with the company's valuation of stock and work in progress – it is definitely overstated."

Three days later, the company accountant committed suicide by jumping off the Clifton suspension bridge, a favourite spot for those who seek to prematurely end their life. The accountant had been colluding with the site foreman who had been ordering construction materials and then diverting them to his house before selling them and splitting the proceeds with his lady friend, the accountant.

STARTING IN BUSINESS

Two years later I realised my ambition to work for myself when I launched my own accountancy business. With assistance from another accountant who gave me some subcontract work, I worked as many hours for him as I could while at the same time seeking to find my own clients. After three months I employed a part-time secretary who I knew from church and the business moved into an office.

We were soon gaining new clients as bank managers were happy to recommend the new kid on the block. As we grew, we hired staff but then there was a two-month period when we won no new clients. No matter what marketing I did or who I spoke with, the phone didn't ring with any enquiries. As Christine left at lunch time, I told her that I had been praying for new clients. I had tried everything else; why not try praying I thought. The next morning I couldn't wait for Christine to arrive so I could tell her that we had three calls and would be engaging three new clients. From that day I started to apply my faith to my business and my finances.

BUDGET DAY

Over the next twenty five years I built three businesses including a publishing company and an Internet business. The publishing company's activities included publishing Budget reports which we wrote immediately after the Chancellor's annual Budget statement. These reports were ordered by accountants to send to their clients and our role was to preprint the firm's details on the covers ready for Budget day. On Budget day we would print hundreds of thousands of reports and then on the finishing lines they were collated with the preprinted front covers and then despatched overnight to accountants' offices. After our first year we grew to the extent that the trimming of the covers was outsourced by our printer. If Andy, the managing director of the print company, had known the trimming company would go into liquidation hours after he had delivered the covers, he would not have let his vans leave the premises.

With 24 hours to go before the Budget, the covers were behind locked doors. No matter who I contacted or what we did the factory doors remained locked. My mind was in overdrive and a state of panic as I knew that if we didn't deliver the reports we would be sued by hundreds of accountants and the business which had enjoyed a meteoric start would be doomed.

I had exhausted every avenue – we all had and by this time there were about 20 staff from our two companies outside the factory. Then, I announced to everyone that I was going to do a 'Joshua' and walk around the factory seven times and ask God to open the doors. No one who was there will ever forget that day. I walked around the factory – each circuit took about two minutes. I prayed all the way; in the state I was in, praying was easy. After six laps I knew the ultimate lap was around the corner and as I walked I prayed more earnestly than before. Everyone else sat there worried – I had gone beyond that! As I came around the corner for the seventh time a car drove up to the factory gate and stopped. The driver jumped out and said "I know what has happened to you, this is not your problem and it's not fair. I am going to open the doors for ten minutes, take your covers out – that's all the time you can have."

That left a deep impression on Andy, the managing director of the print company, and Sheila my co-director. Me? I just know I serve a God who is truly amazing and cares for us individually.

BOUGHT

Financial insights

INTRODUCTION

We all have memories that will last forever; maybe you have a memory from your childhood days? For some it may have been a special holiday, one of the athletes winning an Olympic gold medal. Or for others, the death of Princess Diana. One of my memories is way back in 1966 watching England win the football World Cup. Interestingly, a less memorable event occurred that year as it was also the time the Barclaycard credit card was first introduced in the UK.

The end of the Second World War in 1945 left the country in a situation where a lot of social and property infrastructure required rebuilding. Taxes previously directed toward the war effort were soon to be redirected into rebuilding bombed cities. But taxes were inadequate and with the war debt still outstanding more governmental debt was incurred to rebuild the country, in many instances from the foundations upward. In 1946, the then UK Government introduced the welfare state.

Freedom from war was followed by a desire by those who had lived through those six years to rebuild their lives. Children, jobs, leisure time, aspirations of success and of financial liberty were just some of the objectives held dear by those who had lost family and friends and who held memories they wished to somehow move on from.

Financial institutions such as banks and building societies played their part. In those days it was the building societies' role to lend so enabling people to buy their own property, while banks set about lending to businesses to enable them to grow again, and in so doing creating jobs and wealth.

FAST FORWARD

Government revenue from taxes continued to increase during the eight post war decades. Now, expenditure on the welfare state is measured in hundreds of billions of pounds and accounts for about one third of all government expenditure. Government debt is seemingly a never ending topic of political debate as government wrestles with endeavouring to balance the country's 'household' budget. The words 'austerity measures' are oft heard and have been translated into lost jobs for some. As a country there is a difference of opinion as to whether government spending should be cut quickly or over time. By how much should state spending be reduced given that cuts are seen as reducing welfare benefits or costing jobs? That is but one of the many questions debated by politicians, economists and yes, you and I! One fact is undeniable – if debt increases it may well be future generations who are called on to repay. In the meantime the cost of interest on UK Government debt is over £500 p.a. for every person in this country (HM Treasury forecasts, 2016).

The assumption is that this 'problem' has a solution. But that could be an invalid proposition – at least if we maintain current thinking. No, that is not a political observation but rather a biblical one. Maybe man has so transgressed the laws and counsel of the Bible that there is a price to pay? After all, is not Solomon considered one of the wisest men of old and was he not one of the wealthiest men of Bible times? He is recognised as the author of Proverbs and Ecclesiastes, books that include some great financial wisdom.

MENTION OF AUSTERITY

The global financial crisis gave resonance to a number of financial terms which reverberated for some time in the lexicon of financial commentators. Remember 2007 and the early days of the financial crash when it was referred to as the 'credit crunch'? Very soon banks were owning up to bad lending which was collectively referred to as 'toxic debt'. The credit crunch soon morphed into a fully blown 'global financial crisis'. Then many countries, especially in Europe, sought to reduce government spending through a range of austerity measures. They were, of course, unpopular. After all, why would anyone welcome changes that threatened their life style, notwithstanding most people recognising that government borrowing needs to be aligned with state income?

A FEW OBSERVATIONS

- On the evidence of the first two decades of the twenty-first century, it is hard to dispute that 'man's economy' has its weaknesses and failings. Debt, as we will consider later, has taken a stranglehold and so much of financial policy focuses on deficit reduction – but still government debt increases.

- If we draw conclusions from the behaviour of banks, MPs with their inflated expense claims, and company bosses with their bonus awards, we might conclude that a core component of our financial system is greed.

- Those retired or within ten years of retiring probably have less projected income than they once expected.

- Students face repaying large student loans – that never used to be the case.

- Welfare costs rise as we live longer. That remains the case even after deferring the state pension age.

- In our modern day consumerist society we are all encouraged to buy 'stuff' because we deserve it. And it is so very easy – just take out the card...unlike in days gone by when cash ruled and when there was no money, well there was no money.

- Rampant inflation in 2022/23 caused major problems with inflation peaking at over 10%. The cost of living crisis has created pressure on households as mortgage rates climbed before subsiding in 2024.

Some would suggest that man's economy has failed. I would agree based on the fault lines that have been so clearly exposed.

The good news is that God has an economic plan and it is one that has never and will never fail. It is revealed piece by piece in the Bible. You may know a lot about man's economy but how much do you really know about God's economic plan?

FROM BIG PICTURE TO AN IMPORTANT PICTURE

How do you feel about your finances? How connected are you to the state of your finances? Do you have a spending plan (our term in **Bought** for that which some call their 'budget') that is balanced according to your income? You may feel financially challenged, and probably recognise that you are not the only one. Let's take a quick look at personal finances in this country.

Since the introduction of the credit card we have gone from very little unsecured debt to a position where the average unsecured debt per adult exceed £3,000 – and that is an average; many have no such debt. Do you know how much you owe on cards and consumer credit agreements? Visit yourmoneycounts.org for more up-to-date information.

CREDIT CARDS - PROFIT IS WHAT IT IS ALL ABOUT

The ultimate objective of any commercial organisation is to make a profit. And credit card companies never fail to do that.

The day our children were 18, the credit card application forms started to arrive. How attractive and seductive some of those enticements looked! Offers of interest-free periods, offers of loans. Skilled marketers know how to entice prospects to become customers. When my son attended Fresher's Week he was invited to have a credit card to 'make buying books and coffee easy.' On another occasion he received a letter with a cheque from a credit card company – all he had to do was bank it.

There are now more credit cards in circulation than there are people in this country.

When you access an online game or perhaps buy one, your first task is to find the rules, read them and then follow them. The company that created the game make up the rules. If you have unsecured debt does it ever feel like that to you? The lender makes up the rules – that includes the interest rate and repayment terms. They decide on the charges for late payment – you pay if you are one small step out of line with your monthly payment.

And the rate of interest they charge on your debt? Even with today's low base rate of interest, many of the credit card companies are charging interest rates of 18 per cent or more. That is more than 16 per cent above the Bank of England bank rate.

When I first opened a bank account almost every transaction was made by cheque. Today, there are probably no more than two cheque entries on any one statement. Plastic or mobile has become the primary means of exchange, notwithstanding the fact there are those who only use cash. Most transactions that pass directly onto my account are made via debit card, while my credit card has an automatic direct debit payment mechanism that results in my month's purchases being charged to my bank account.

With the ability to make payments now so automatic and electronic, it is easy to become detached from the outstanding debt that for so many increases almost unnoticed. Years ago banks used to use red ink to indicate an overdrawn balance – now everything is 'in the black'.

PENSIONERS IN DEBT

It is easy to assume it is those approaching middle age who are the ones most burdened with debt. While that may well be so, this group may also include parents who are deep in the grip of debt. Retirees are not only retiring in debt but as many as 30 per cent are reported to have taken out more loans to cope with rising living costs. On average this debt exceeds £30,000 but 1 in 10 find themselves owing more than £100,000. Maybe the debt of pensioners gives some insight as to why the generations that follow have similarly become accustomed to relying on debt. Many have failed to repay the mortgage and enter retirement in debt to their mortgage lender.

16 – 25 YEAR OLDS

A survey of those aged 16 to 25 called 'Penny for your thoughts' exploring young peoples' relationships with and attitudes toward finance shows that:

- only 6% of respondents said they manage their money by sticking to a fixed spending plan

- two in ten (22%) said they just cross their fingers and hope they don't run out of cash

- more than two thirds (68%) of respondents had been encouraged to take out credit they either did not want or could not afford

- a third (34%) of the young people that completed the survey had debt-related problems at the time, and a further 13% had done in the past.

According to the survey, millions of teenagers are planning to fund their lifestyle through credit cards, overdrafts and loans. As many as 44% of 16 to 17 year olds are planning to take out a credit card when they become an adult; 18% are thinking of taking out a bank loan when they turn 18, and a further 17% expect to be overdrawn.

Is it really a good situation that man's economy is being installed into the everyday practices of our young people?

STUDENT LOANS

Starting in 1990/91 with a maximum loan of £420 these loans increased to a maximum of just over £13,000 in 2024. Lending amounts to £10 billion per annum with an average loan at the end of higher education in excess of £45,000. Currently there is in excess of £200 billion outstanding. Many students leave higher education with student debt in excess of £45,000 and have to factor in repayments, which in the early years of working often do not even cover the cost of interest.

CONSOLIDATION LOANS - NEW DEBT FOR OLD?

Watching daytime television a few years ago I was amazed to see how many advertisements there were for debt consolidation loans. What do I think of consolidation loans? Personally, I dislike them intensely and in my role as an accountant and financial adviser would always hesitate to advocate using them. In my opinion, the clue to the real nature of these loans is in their name, CONsolidation. A CONsolidation loan is usually used to pay off all unsecured debts and creates a new loan account. Sometimes people add in extra cash borrowing. These loans combine debts (which probably have varying interest rates and term periods) into one loan with one monthly payment. Sometimes loans have a penalty clause for early repayment which is triggered on consolidation.

The net effect is normally threefold:

1. The length of time to repay is stretched, and so
2. The monthly repayments reduce, and so
3. The total interest paid increases compared to what you would have paid, and as a result...

...many people who consolidate their debts in this way find they have spare cash each month and start to spend it and then...the new balance on the credit card doesn't get paid off at the end of the month. The cycle of debt has begun again. In fact it is estimated that the majority of people who take out a consolidation loan actually end up in further debt.

PAYDAY LOANS

Conversely, payday lenders aim to lend primarily in the short term. Their rates are exorbitant, ranging up to 1,500 per cent, maybe even more. Payday loans average somewhere in the region of £250, with almost all loans less than £1,000. Rates are now very much lower – at one point in 2012 rates from Wonga exceeded 6,000 per cent. In 2024 it is reported that the average interest rate is in the 1500 per cent region. AVOID at all costs - these are usury rates of interest.

Thankfully, following God's economy will keep you from being caught in the trap of these companies.

WAYS IN WHICH WE ARE PERSUADED TO SPEND MONEY

With more than £1,000 spent on marketing for every adult in this country there are always spending opportunities for us to contemplate. It would be quite easy to write a book on spending temptations, so I have decided to highlight a few that appear to be optional, unnecessary and in some cases addictive.

1. ONLINE GAMBLING

There are now thousands of websites dedicated to online gambling. These sites often use the word 'gaming' in order to avoid the word 'gambling'. It is reckoned that more than 70 per cent of gaming is now online with 4 per cent of teens having a gaming problem. One dad came up to me in church to tell me how worried he was that he had found out that his son was addicted to online gaming. In fact pathological gaming is recognised as a clinical disorder. The offers of free gambling money are there to entice you to spend (or should I say, lose) your hard-earned money. Remember, the people who make up the rules win. You only have to look at pictures of Las Vegas hotels and casinos to know that the owners of gambling establishments have the odds well and truly stacked in their favour. How addictive is online gambling? Very; the average young person is estimated to spend 10,000 hours gaming by the time they reach the age of 21.

2. TV PHONE-INS

Now, maybe by this point, you think I am a killjoy. Not so, but the TV companies have admitted rigging competitions so that they could profiteer from your calls. How much do you spend on this in a year?

3. TV SHOPPING CHANNELS

I have fleetingly watched these channels with interest although never been tempted to buy more 'stuff'. It seems that more than 80% of what they sell is only going to appeal to those who wish to buy on impulse. There is an endless focus on what the product could do for you and how you will look, accompanied by 'the saving' they offer. But, you have to spend to save. It might even be possible to go broke by saving so much money!

4. INTERNET SPENDING

Like the television it is so easy to click and spend. I use the internet to buy those products that I have to buy. I cannot recall ever buying any 'stuff' as a result of website advertisements. I recall my daughter telling me she used to pay as much as £10 a month for ringtones. That is probably one reason why I decided to be careful with my own click and spend habits.

5. WATCH OUT THERE ARE CHARGES ABOUT

Banks and credit card companies have been taken to task regarding their practice of high charges when an account goes overdrawn or a payment is made late. I recall a newspaper story that recounted how one bank had managed to make one person's unauthorised overdraft of £10 into a debt of more than £350. When ordering online there are sometimes hidden charges that are only advised at the end of the transaction.

YOUR FINANCES ARE NOT SECURE

In one two-year period my credit card was subject to fraud three times while my bank managed to resurrect a credit card account that had been closed three years previously and then charge me £80 for their 'error'. Now, with bank and credit card payment systems dominated by automatic charges, it is essential to keep track of payments on your accounts, either online or by text. There are many people dedicated to fraud who are seeking to access your accounts. We all need to be aware of the significant threat posed by identity fraud. It is almost impossible to be over-diligent, but it is very easy to miss fraudulent transactions unless you check carefully the payments charged to your accounts. It is also important to keep your receipts so you can check these against your statements of account.

SAVINGS

Many have inadequate savings for retirement, to the point where some people believe that they will just have to continue working to live. Changes in pension legislation have enabled many to access their funds – but will they have what is required when they are five or more years into retirement? The retirement shortfall statistics are normally reported as being in the billions, and if you are like me, you switch over to working out what that means for you. We work for maybe 75,000 hours or more in our lifetime to have the prospect of a retirement that enables us to decide what to do with our time. A reward for all that hard work? Well, that might be what some achieve, but sadly there are a good proportion of pensioners for whom that is not the case.

HOW HAS THIS HAPPENED?

Those retiring today are sometimes referred to as the 'baby boomers' – those who went on their first European package holiday, enjoyed a higher standard of living than their parents and had greater expectations regarding the quality of life. The relaxation of credit in the 1970s, our increasing affluence, the advance of choice and consumerism, and the exponential growth of credit since the 1990s, have contributed to a society that relies in part on debt.

WHAT IS THE ANSWER?

Some look to government – but based on the past it is hard to see any significant solution coming from Parliament. The answer probably isn't new, but a combination of options. Will there be a return to selling the parental home and moving in with children? We have moved away from this in recent years, but it is commonplace in some European countries.

For those who are empty nesters, downsizing is one option. Continuing to work part-time is another. Subject to the economy, there are often jobs that are geared towards pensioners looking for additional income. Pensioners also come with advantages, such as experience.

Maybe more will access equity release schemes, but great care is needed if this is being considered. Some who thought this was the best course of action have regretted their actions a few years later.

What about those who are younger? How will those fare who are paying so much more for their properties than was the case for today's pensioners? For many who are saddled with debt today, contemplating how retirement will look is probably far too remote a scenario. Having to cope with the cost of living is about as much as many can think about.

We could dissect the state of our finances in more depth. There are many who write and analyse the state of the nation's finances on the internet or in the weekend newspapers. Your money counts to you and probably those close to you. The world's economy is in a mess. Some of those institutions that have been responsible for sub-prime loans, extending credit and unsecured loans, selling financial products that weren't necessary, have themselves mismanaged their company finances. As a result they ask shareholders for money to bail them out of their predicament. Some are required to pay fines for their misdemeanours.

However, if you find yourself at a point where nothing else has worked, take heart: God loves you and His Word never fails. He has bought you at a price because of that love. We will outline simple practical steps you can pursue in order to make lasting changes to managing your own finances.

Your Money Counts is a Christian charity that aims to unlock people's understanding of what the Bible has to say, with practical applications for money and possessions. **Bought** is a cornerstone book that provides an overview and insight into what God has to say about the handling of our finances.

Visit yourmoneycounts.org for additional help information and guidance.

The Problem

ONE COUPLE'S MOMENT OF TRUTH

Jonathan and Helen decided to end their marriage of 11 years. Their relationship had been difficult for some time. Arguments were commonplace and a couple who were once so close found themselves, at times, almost at war with one another. The truth is that although it was not the only area where they argued, money, or the lack of it, seemed to come up often.

In anticipation of the divorce settlement, Jonathan began to review the family's financial position. As he sorted through the files, he came across an old faded invoice from the hotel where he and Helen had stayed on their honeymoon. Another receipt was for an instalment on their first car. He picked up still another invoice and remembered with fatherly pride how he had paid for a school trip to France for their second child. And then there was the deposit payment on their first home, the credit card receipts for their first child's cot, the family's annual zoo entrance subscription and the payment to tour Buckingham Palace....

After several hours of sorting through such papers, Jonathan realised how much he and his wife had invested in their marriage. He paused, deep in thought for several minutes. Then he closed the file and called his wife on her mobile. After an awkward exchange he blurted out the reason for his call. Would she work with him to rebuild their marriage? He recognised where he had been at fault and wanted to do everything possible to make the marriage work.

While a family crisis such as Jonathan and Helen's may be alien to some of us, the message of their family's payments is common. It is the story of our lives. It tells us about our values, our priorities, our memories, how much we save, what we spend money on, to whom we give. In fact, our bank and credit card statements tell us more about our priorities than anything else.

YOUR SITUATION

There are a number of aspects of life that we think about every day – food and relationships are obvious ones, so too is the handling of our money and possessions.

Are you:

- Having enough or not having enough?
- Facing unexpected costs?
- Losing a job?
- Unable to work due to an accident or ill health?
- Are living costs increasing more than income?
- A business unable to provide the necessary income?
- Are you unable to repay loans?
- Is Credit card spending out of control?
- Is there any unnecessary spending?
- Does a partner with a secret account?

WHOSE ADVICE DO YOU SEEK?

There may come a point when desperation results in a call for help. It may be that you seek to sort things out yourself. Payday lender? Consolidation loans? As we discussed in the previous chapter, these are not necessarily the best options. Visit to the bank? Maybe, but it depends what the nature of the problem is. In the book of Proverbs we read that "the way of a fool seems right to them, but the wise listen to advice" (Proverbs 12:15). But from whom? Well one source of wise counsel that the Bible talks about is from the Lord himself. Psalms tells us that "I will instruct you and teach you in the way you should go; I will counsel you with my loving eye on you" (Psalm 32:8). The Bible is our manufacturer's handbook, the only book God has ever written. Let's start to look at what we might find in the Bible to help us address and solve any financial problem.

But first let's address any thoughts you might have if you think you do not have what we might describe as a 'problem.' You might not be in debt. You might have a comfortable lifestyle and be able to afford anything you want. On the face of it you do not have an obvious problem. But dig a little deeper and challenge yourself as to whether you are following God's economic blueprint.

So, if you do recognise you have a problem you will discover in Part 2 how following God's Word will help you.

If you don't think you have a problem then use **Bought** as a checklist and see how you are really doing.

And, whichever category you place yourself in, recognise that God loves you, is for you and will be with you at all times.

Let's look at the Bible's credentials in the area of our finances...

THE BIBLE – AN AMAZING INSIGHT INTO GOD'S ECONOMIC PLAN

God is our Creator and the Bible is our Creator's handbook. It is the only book He wrote and it tells His story. There are 31,102 verses, and within those we find 2,350 that give advice and instruction on how we should handle our money, wealth and possessions. Jesus tells 38 stories in the New Testament to illustrate something He wished to teach; the Bible refers to these stories as 'parables'. Of these, 16 relate to how we handle our money, wealth and possessions; in fact 15% of Jesus' recorded words are on this subject. Indeed, the Bible says more about money and possessions than about almost any subject other than God himself and the cross. The Bible offers 500 verses on prayer while fewer than 500 discuss faith. There are 700 verses directly about the handling of money and 300 about our responsibility to the poor.

> *There are 31,102 verses and within those we find 2,350 that give advice and instruction on how we should handle our money, wealth and possessions.*

The Lord Jesus said a lot about money and possessions because He wants us to know His perspective on this critical area of our life. He deals with financial matters because money does matter. There are so many that want to have a say in how we manage our finances, whether it is in offering to extend credit or helping us save or spend. In fact they shout so loudly we can hardly hear ourselves think! But it is important that we have the first word and the last word on what we do with our money. Western economies revolve around the world's system of spending and buying. We should be prepared to challenge the view that we are to live for today without too much of an eye on the future, that debt is desirable, affordable and necessary and that investing is impossible when household finances are under such pressure. Your financial views may include one or more of these positions. Television and media commentators periodically focus intensely on the latest financial crisis, whatever they or government perceive that to be.

The Bible sets out God's perspective on how we should handle our finances and possessions. You may find most of what you will read obvious, but this may not always be the case. Where you find something that you consider obvious and relevant to you, ask yourself: "Am I doing it?" When you read something you are not doing, then ask: "Do I agree?" God's economy differs fundamentally from that of the world. Why? Because God has an eternal perspective – not a 'spend and have or experience today' perspective.

God is the Creator and the Creator who created all things: "in the beginning God created the heavens and the earth" (Genesis 1:1). Colossians 1:16 reads, "For by Him all things were created, both in the heavens and on earth, visible and invisible, whether thrones or dominions or rulers or authorities - all things have been created through Him and for Him."

This knowledge and insight from the Bible has helped millions of people in their Christian life to align their finances in accordance with biblical principles.

Applying these principles is crucial for three reasons:

1. HOW WE HANDLE MONEY AFFECTS OUR FELLOWSHIP WITH THE LORD

In Luke 16:11 we read: "if you have not been trustworthy in handling worldly wealth, who will trust you with true riches?"

In this verse Jesus links how we handle our money with the quality of our spiritual life. If we handle our money properly according to the principles of Scripture, our fellowship with Christ will grow stronger. However, if we manage money unfaithfully, our fellowship with Him will suffer.

Someone once told me that the Lord often allows a person to teach a subject because he or she needs to develop and mature in that area. That has certainly been true for me in the area of money. I have had the privilege of counselling hundreds of people and leading many small groups. I have known many people who testify to how they have changed their attitude to money and have experienced a meaningful improvement in their fellowship with the Lord.

While in the midst of updating this book, I took a phone call from someone who shared how, while reading it they had completely changed how they think about finances and how they communicate with their spouse. The call lasted about 30 minutes and all I did was listen and thank God for the power of His Word and of the Holy Spirit, and, for the soft heart that listened to what God has to say.

2. POSSESSIONS COMPETE WITH THE LORD

Possessions are a primary competitor with Christ for lordship of our lives. Jesus tells us we must choose to serve only one of two masters: "No-one can serve two masters. Either he will hate the one and love the other, or he will be devoted to the one and despise the other. You cannot serve both God and money" (Matthew 6:24). It is impossible for us to serve money – even in a small way – and still serve the Lord.

When the Crusades were being fought during the 12th century, the crusaders employed mercenaries to fight on their behalf. Because it was a religious war, the crusaders insisted that the mercenaries be baptised before fighting. As they were being baptised, the mercenaries would hold their swords out of the water to symbolise the one thing in their life that Jesus Christ did not control. They had the freedom to use the swords in any way they wished. How wrong that was. Today many people handle their money in a similar fashion, though they may not be as obvious about it. They hold their wallet or purse or card 'out of the water', in effect saying, "God, You can be the Lord of my entire life except for my money. I am perfectly capable of handling that myself."

3. MUCH OF LIFE REVOLVES AROUND THE USE OF MONEY

During your normal week, how much time do you spend earning money in your job, making decisions on how to spend money, thinking about where to save and invest money or praying about your giving? Fortunately, God has prepared us adequately for these tasks by giving us the Bible as His blueprint for handling money.

THE ANSWER

With the twenty-first century seeing so much financial upheaval, people increasingly wonder where they can turn for help. There are two basic alternatives: the Bible or the answers people devise. The way most people handle money is in sharp contrast to God's financial principles. Isaiah 55:8 reads, "For my thoughts are not your thoughts, neither are your ways my ways, declares the Lord" (NKJV).

LEARNING TO BE CONTENT

When contentment is mentioned in the Bible, it more often than not refers to money. In Philippians 4:11-13 Paul writes, "I have learned to be content whatever the circumstances. I know what it is to be in need, and I know what it is to have plenty. I have learned the secret of being content in any and every situation, whether well fed or hungry, whether living in plenty or in want. I can do everything through Him who gives me strength."

Examine these verses carefully. We are not born with the instinct for contentment; rather it is learned.

The intention of **Bought** is to provide an overview of what can be learnt from the Bible about handling money and possessions. We will offer you practical ways to integrate these principles into your life. You don't have to be an accountant to implement these principles. Paul tells us in 2 Timothy 3:16 that, "All Scripture is God-breathed and is useful for teaching, rebuking, correcting and training in righteousness, so that the man of God may be thoroughly equipped for every good work." As you discover these principles and put them into practice, you will draw closer to Christ, submit more fully to Him as Lord, learn to be content, and set your financial house in order.

Consider this

An introduction: issues and problems

GET MORE INSIGHTS AT
→ WWW.YOURMONEYCOUNTS.ORG.UK

The world has a lot to say about how we manage our finances. So too does the Lord.

The world's economy never seems to be stable. Following God's biblical financial principles provides a godly solution to an area that so many find challenging.

Relationships are enhanced or degraded based on how we handle money. This is particularly true of marriage relationships.

It is important for Christians to resist the pull of the culture and to take great care when it comes to increasing levels of debt.

Christians should live lives of intentionality – that is especially true when it comes to the handling of our money and possessions.

Key Questions:

Do you have a written, God-inspired financial plan that you follow?

What have you learned in Part 1 and how will you apply this to your situation?

What do you think Luke 16: 11 means – what are the 'true riches'?

List the areas where you think the handling of your finances falls short and pray that the Lord will reveal His will and wisdom into your situation.

Would your family find what you are learning of interest? If so, share what you are learning – as you receive be prepared to give out of your own God-inspired wisdom. Be prayerful and humble in matters appertaining to finance as these are usually sensitive.

The Bible: A blueprint for living

2

Ownership | Stewardship

We are called to be faithful managers. That is not easy in a society that is materialistic and encourages the acquisition of possessions which can compromise our ability to be faithful in our service of Him and others. We are called to live a life with an eternal perspective and for our hearts and minds to be transformed.

A young baby soon gets to grip with ownership – especially when there is an older sibling around. But we also need to beware as we are also conditioned to think of possessions as 'mine'.

Ownership

On one occasion I was addressing a group of about 100 people who were all involved in teaching biblical financial principles to Christians. I started with this question: "How many of you own a business?" Almost all of those that were in business put their hands up. At which point I repeated the question with emphasis on the word 'own'. The penny dropped. Whatever you commit to, it is first nature to think of that which you possess as **yours**. In the case of a business owner, it is their time, expertise, capital that has gone into building the business – their sweat, blood and tears.

The home you live in – do you not refer to that as **your** home? **Your** car? **Your** children?

Discovering what the Bible has to say about God's ownership came as something as a surprise to me – as indeed does quite a lot of the instruction in the Bible that revolves around the handling of money and possessions. I was the founder of three companies and always regarded them as my companies; why would I have considered that they belonged to God? In fact, I do find that gaining a deep understanding of God's ownership is key to changing attitudes and practices in all matters financial.

As those who love the Lord, Christians have a personal relationship with the Jesus Christ and also have the inner presence of the Holy Spirit for guidance. We also have the Bible and that is not just about the stories and characters of the Old Testament, the wisdom of Solomon, the praises of David or the sufferings of Job. Neither is the New Testament just about the life of Jesus, the travels and letters of Paul or the story of the End Times.

Throughout the Bible there are lessons to be learnt and applied. Lessons about handling adversity, addressing anxiety, dealing with grief, developing integrity, being honest, loving, mentoring, obedience, serving, suffering, wisdom, work, fear, loneliness, humility, having hope, being joyful, parenting, being part of a church, God's love, marriage, worship, forgiveness, eternal life, salvation, courage, commitment, choices, identity, unity, faith, contentment, prayer, belief, and that is only a partial list. However, if you had to create a list of the top ten Bible topics then there are more verses about God than any other topic followed by all matters pertaining to the handling of money and possessions, of which there are 2,350 verses.

So, why so many? Maybe God knew that this is an aspect of our lives that would represent a major area of challenge, and so when the Holy Spirit inspired the Bible authors He gave us a blueprint for how to handle finances God's way.

When I was first introduced to what the Bible had to say about finance and possessions it caused me to look back over my life and examine how my handling of finances compared to what the Bible had to say. I had given – but not as generously as perhaps I should have done. I had an early bad experience with card debt in the form of revolving credit and decided that 'debt was dumb'.

With my wife's help we had managed our household finances fairly well, given our children a modicum of understanding about handling money, and made a commitment to save. When starting the first of 'my' three businesses (one of my companies operated two separate businesses) I decided to only take out the minimum and ensure that the business retained enough to pay taxes, invest in growth and have a cushion in the event of something unexpected.

Looking back, I concluded that the prompting of the Holy Spirit must have kept this biblically financially uneducated person somewhat in line with the Bible.

So, in my mid-fifties I learnt for the first time that God owns everything. I had read at least two of the verses that tell us this very clearly. But evidently I had not understood clearly enough. Guess what I discovered? These verses appeared in both the Old and New Testaments: Psalm 24:1 reads, "The earth is the Lord's, and everything in it the world, and all who live in it," and an abbreviated form of this verse appears in 1 Corinthians 10:26: "The earth is the Lord's, and everything in it." I was struck by the words 'everything' and 'all'. There was no doubt about it, no wriggle room, no denying what the Bible was telling me. They were never my businesses after all and neither was my house really mine.

OUR OWNERSHIP OR HIS LORDSHIP?

If we seek to be true followers of Christ, we must acknowledge His ownership and act accordingly. Jesus told His disciples "those of you who do not give up everything you have cannot be my disciples" (Luke 14:33). Sometimes He tests us by asking us to give up the very possessions that are most important to us.

The most vivid example of this concerns Abraham who was instructed "take your son, your only son, whom you love— Isaac—and go to the region of Moriah. Sacrifice him there as a burnt offering on a mountain I will show you" (Genesis 22:2). Abraham obeyed, demonstrating his willingness to give up his most valuable possession. God responded "Do not lay a hand on the boy, and do not do anything to him. Now I know that you fear God, because you have not withheld from me your son, your only son" (Genesis 22:12).

When we acknowledge God's ownership, every spending decision becomes a spiritual decision. No longer do we ask "Lord, what do you want me to do with my money?" It becomes "Lord, what do You want me to do with Your money?" When we have this attitude and handle His money according to His wishes, spending and saving decisions become as spiritual as giving decisions.

GOD'S PART AS OWNER

The Lord did not design people to shoulder the responsibilities that only He can carry. Jesus said "Come to me, all you who are weary and burdened, and I will give you rest. Take my yoke upon you.... For My yoke is easy and my burden is light" (Matthew 11: 28-30).

For most of us, the primary problem is failing to consistently recognise God's part. Our culture believes that God plays no part in financial matters, and we have, in some measure, been influenced by that view.

The Lord's ownership influences how we care for possessions. For example, because the Lord is the owner of where we live, we want to please Him by keeping His home cleaner and in better repair!

ONE ASPECT OF REMINDING YOU WHO THE OWNER REALLY IS

I am probably slower in my thinking than others but the fact is it took me at least three months before I could fully accept that God owns everything. In fact I now have a spreadsheet that lists out my various investments; allow me to share with you what I am worth: the bottom line of my spreadsheet tells me that I am worth **nothing**. How can that be? I have simply made that spreadsheet conform to the Bible – the penultimate line reads: 'Deduct [value of line above] as this all belongs to God'.

Stewardship

The Bible makes it clear that we are stewards of that which we possess. A steward is a manager of someone else's property. The Lord has given us authority to be stewards. "You made them rulers over the works of your hands; You put everything under their feet" (Psalm 8:6). Think of it another way. As a landlord owns the property, so the tenant who occupies the property has certain rights and responsibilities. A 'tenancy' is another way of looking at stewardship.

So, how easy is it to make the change in mindset from being an owner to being a steward? I don't think it is easy at all. Look at the 18-month old child who has a slightly older sibling. As previously mentioned, the younger child is starting to recognise that some of those toys belong in their hands and then the older sibling decides to play with the younger one's toy. The younger child starts to well up with what amounts to anger – "my sister has my toy" is a thought process that is evidently clear from the other side of the room! Very soon the tears of anguish start to flow, and they do not cease until the parent has rescued what belongs to the youngest. A few months later the child has learnt the words 'mum' and 'dad' and now starts to enhance their vocabulary. As natural as those first two words are so are some of the next and 'mine' is sure to be a word that when yelled with gusto, results in the toy being returned and the eldest going off in something of a huff. You see ownership is in our DNA. It's a 'what's mine is mine' belief system. Does that evaporate over time? I think maybe - but often with some difficulty. Think about it: if someone steals something from you, or perhaps you lend a tool or a piece of equipment and it is not returned – you really do want it back. That sense of ownership is there, isn't it?

God has rights as owner, and we have responsibilities as stewards. As we look at these it is important to remember that God has shown His love for us and He is a God rich in mercy and grace. He has given us these principles because He wants the best for us. Most people discover areas in which they have not been obedient to the Word. Please don't become discouraged. Going forward simply seek to apply faithfully what you learn from God's word.

Here are a few areas to consider and ways to demonstrate our faithfulness:

1. FAITHFUL WITH ALL OUR RESOURCES

We are charged to be faithful in handling 100 per cent of our income. We are not taught or do not know how to handle money on a biblical basis; many Christians have wrong attitudes about possessions and make incorrect financial decisions that lead to painful consequences. Hosea 4:6 reads "my people are destroyed from lack of knowledge". Ignorance of (or disobedience to) scriptural financial principles frequently causes money problems.

2. FAITHFUL, REGARDLESS OF HOW MUCH WE HAVE

The issue is how to handle faithfully all that God has entrusted to us. The faithful steward is responsible for what he or she has, whether it is much or little. The parable of the talents illustrates this. "It will be like a man going on a journey, who called his servants and entrusted his property to them. To one he gave five talents of money, to another two talents, and to another one talent, each according to his ability" (Matthew 25:14-15). When the master returned, he held each slave accountable for managing his possessions faithfully. The master commended the faithful slave who received the five talents: "Well done, good and faithful servant! You have been faithful with a few things; I will put you in charge of many things. Come and share your master's happiness!" (Matthew 25:21). Interestingly, the slave who had been given two talents received a reward equal to that given to the slave who had been given the five talents (see Matthew 25:23). We are required to be faithful whether we are given much or little. As someone once said: "It's not what I would do if one million pounds were my lot; it's what I am doing with the ten pounds I've got." Wealth is not equally distributed. Around half the world's population lives on less than £1 a day, while the purchasing power of that money is much less than £5. So, if you have £5 to spend on whatever you choose you probably rank as one of the wealthiest people in the world!

3. FAITHFULNESS IN LITTLE THINGS

Luke 16:10 reads, "Whoever can be trusted with very little can also be trusted with much, and whoever is dishonest with very little will also be dishonest with much". How do you know if a young adult is going to take good care of his first car? Observe how he cared for his bicycle. How do you know if a salesperson will do a competent job of serving a large client? Observe how he or she serves a small client. If we have the character to be faithful with small things, the Lord knows He can trust us with greater responsibilities.

"Small things are small things," Hudson Taylor, the missionary statesman, said "but faithfulness with a small thing is a big thing."

4. FAITHFULNESS WITH ANOTHER'S POSSESSIONS

Faithfulness with another's possessions will, in some measure, determine the amount with which you are entrusted. "And if you have not been trustworthy with someone else's property, who will give you property of your own?" (Luke 16:12). This is a principle that is often overlooked. Are you faithful with another's possessions? Are you careless with your employer's office supplies? Do you waste electricity when you are staying in a hotel room? When someone allows you to use something, are you careful to return it in good condition?

5. FAITHFULNESS BUILDS CHARACTER

God uses money to refine our character. In 1918 David McConaughy wrote a book, **Money, the Acid Test**. In it he said:

Money, most common of temporal things, involves uncommon and eternal consequences. Even though it may be done quite unconsciously, money molds people – in the process of getting it, of saving it, of using it, of giving it, of accounting for it. Depending upon how it is handled, it proves a blessing or a curse to its possessor; either the person becomes master of the money, or the money becomes master of the person. Our Lord takes money, the thing that, essential though it is to our common life, sometimes seems so sordid, and he makes it a touchstone to test the lives of people and an instrument for molding them into the likeness of himself.

Clearly, if we are handling our possessions as faithful stewards, our character is being built. If we are unfaithful, our character is being compromised and harmed. For most of us there are three aspects of our lives which we consider every day:

- health
- relationships, and
- finances.

Jesus Christ said more about money than any other single thing because money is of great importance when it comes to a person's real nature. How we handle money is an exact index to our true character. Throughout Scripture we find an intimate correlation between the development of a person's character and how they handle money.

6. FAITHFULNESS LEADS TO CONTENTMENT

Once we know God's part and our part, and faithfully do our part, we can be content. In Philippians we discover that Paul has learned to be content because he knew that God would supply all his needs: "But my God shall supply all your need according to his riches in glory by Christ Jesus" (Philippians 4:19), and he had been faithful. "Whatever you have learned or received or heard from me, or seen in me – put it into practice" (Philippians 4:9).

As we apply the principles of God's economy, we will begin to get out of debt, spend more wisely, start saving for our future goals and give even more to the work of Christ. The Bible offers real solutions to today's financial problems.

"Come to me, all you who are weary and burdened, and I will give you rest. Take my yoke upon you…. For My yoke is easy and my burden is light."

Matthew 11: 28-30

Consider this

The Bible: A blueprint for living

GET MORE INSIGHTS AT
→ WWW.YOURMONEYCOUNTS.ORG.UK

God owns everything.

When we acknowledge God's ownership spending decisions take on a greater spiritual dimension.

The Lord's ownership should influence how we care for possessions.

We are stewards and should be faithful with all our resources.

Good stewards also practice contentment.

Key questions:
How long do you think it will take for you to accept and act knowing that God owns everything you have?

How have financial challenges shaped your character?

How do you think you could increase your faithfulness?

How can you be more faithful in little things?

What financial challenges do you face that need you to be more faithful?

3

Free to serve Him

Debt | Getting out of debt |
Counsel – seeking Godly wisdom

The Bible makes it clear that debt has always been a challenge and that it represents a serious threat to the peace of mind and freedom of the believer. The distress caused when in debt, no matter how that debt has arisen, causes many to lose hope. But hope is at hand and a solution does exist. Faith and obedience play a part, as does contentment and the need to be disciplined.

———

Debt

THOUSANDS WILL HELP YOU INTO DEBT

The word 'debt' is derived from the Middle English word **dette** and the Latin word debitum – a thing owed. And if there is one word that we hear about over and over again it is the English version 'debt'. The debt of governments or personal debt.

There are thousands of organisations that are willing to extend credit so that goods and services can be purchased, and there are thousands of businesses which are more than happy for people to use these services so that you can have what you want – now!

I will refer later to Proverbs 22:7 which tells us that, "the borrower is slave to the lender."

WHAT IS DEBT?

Lenders and advertisers use attractive euphemisms for debt to entice you into borrowing, masking its harsh reality. I have yet to see one advertisement that promises the good life of 'buy now and pay later' balanced with words that describe the reality of debt. Are you beginning to have the feeling that the 'gospel' of 'buy it because you deserve it' might not be telling the whole truth as you are enduring the pain of all that debt?

Debt is 'a sum of money owed' and includes money owed to credit-card companies, bank loans, money borrowed from relatives, consumer loans, consolidation loans and the home mortgage. Bills that become due in the month, such as any monthly account, (e.g. window cleaning or a repair bill) are not considered debt provided they are paid on time. However, some monthly utility bills may have an outstanding balance that is not covered by the ongoing monthly direct debits, and to that extent there may be debt embedded in these accounts. This occurs when energy costs increase and there is no prompt action to increase the regular utility payments. One course of action here is to contact the utility company and revise payments, for it is better to act sooner rather than later. But if your utility bills are estimated, read your meter and update your supplier to ensure you are not taken unaware by an actual account that is higher than the estimate.

DEBT IS ALL AROUND US

We have so much personal debt in our nation that the average person has been described as someone driving on a debt-financed road, in a bank-financed car, powered by credit card-financed fuel, going to purchase furniture on an instalment plan to put in his mortgage-financed home!

AN IMAGINARY SCENARIO

The end of World War 2 saw churches packed as people prayed for peace and the return of their loved ones. Many had faith in God at their time of need.

I imagine a scenario whereby, one day after the War had ended, Satan sat around with his cohorts to address the 'problem' of there being too many people having faith in God. As he sat around the table he asked for some ideas on how to reverse the love, affection and trust toward God. He asked for ideas. "Satan," a voice was heard "in the Bible it says...

"No, not the Bible – I can't stand that book" the leader said.

"No, listen to me this is really good. In Proverbs it says that the borrower is slave to the lender." The speaker finished and around the room there was a hush.

"Interesting, I like the idea of God's people being slaves – well done, but don't read that book again any time soon will you?"

"Any other ideas?" Satan asked.

"Well there are a lot of people who are getting back together as couples. Lots getting married and oh dear there are so many babies being born. Everyone seems so much in love and happy – it is God's way. Satan just listen to this while a few verses were again quoted …"

"No, no, no – not more from that book again!" By now the raised voice expressed anger as the clenched fist hit the table. "Please listen to me," the anxious voice implored.

"OK, but be quick and it had better be as good if not better than the slavery idea – oh how I like the idea of God's people being slaves."

"Thanks boss." In Romans 7: 2 it says that "by law a married woman is bound to her husband as long as he is alive, but if her husband dies, she is released from the law that binds her to him. So then, if she has sexual relations with another man while her husband is still alive, she is called an adulteress. But if her husband dies, she is released from that law and is not an adulteress if she marries another man." And again in 1 Corinthians 7:5 it even mentions you our leader "Do not deprive one another except with consent for a time, that you may give yourselves to fasting and prayer; and come together again so that Satan does not tempt you because of your lack of self-control."

"Interesting, interesting, I like it a lot. That's it, no more ideas needed. Let debt grow and grow and let's see what we can do to promote unfaithfulness in marriage. In fact we can probably sometimes combine the strategies. You know, people in debt, stress, marriage breakdown. Infidelity. Broken marriages. Children without dads at home. It all makes good sense. Good meeting, let's get on with it and let the mission begin."

> *Out of debt, out of danger*
> *Proverb*

BACK TO BEING MORE SPIRITUAL

Our money and possessions are part of the spiritual battlefield and it is a spiritual war that is being waged – one that we can and must win, and in fact in Christ has already won.

Being free to serve Him comprises a number of foundations including: not being in the grip of debt; being a good steward; being diligent in working, and providing an income for the household, saving and giving. An eye on today, tomorrow and eternity – because how we live in this life determines our rewards in eternity.

A household appliance unexpectedly fails and needs replacing. The car service reveals hundreds of pounds of additional repair costs. Christmas costs far more than expected. The children need this or that. Redundancy…and so on. Some debt is **unplanned**. It arrives because of circumstances such as those just mentioned. Some debt is **planned**. For example: the mortgage, the car loan, perhaps even the credit arrangement on some item of household furniture, or maybe an agreement to spread a cost over a year – insurance is one example. Some debt is **accumulated**. Debt on credit or store cards is a good example. Initially there is every intention of paying off the debt, but as time passes this does not happen, and before you know it, you owe far more than you ever anticipated. "Most of our debts were accumulated so slowly over the years and we just did not realise what was happening until it was too late" was how one person described the couple's seemingly impossible mountain of debt. No matter what you do, the debt never seems to reduce – it just keeps revolving, just as the card companies want it to be.

All debt needs to be repaid. On time! Fail to do so and an avalanche of 'red' [threatening] letters start arriving on the doorstep. Court action may be threatened. Even repossession of your home.

Each year, millions of people find themselves in the debt zone predicament. A credit expert says the major reason is "damage to the borrower's ability to pay". People take out loans on the assumption they will have a steady flow of income, then the unexpected happens. Someone gets sick. State benefits are withdrawn or personal costs increase. A new baby is on the way. An employer goes out of business.

INCREASING DEBT

Government, business and personal debt is exploding in our nation. At over three trillion (that is 3 followed by 12 noughts!) pounds, national and personal debt is more than £45,000 for every UK resident. Mortgage interest is low due to low interest rates, but how much would your mortgage repayment increase by if the interest rate was 2 per cent higher?

With students normally dependent on debt, and with housing, energy and basic living costs at such a high proportion of most people's income, it is not surprising there are many who cannot manage financially. Paying the mortgage or rent is most people's main financial priority. Sometimes there is insufficient money left for settling unsecured monthly debt repayments. There are now more credit cards in circulation today than there are people living in this country. As the number of cars on the road increases so do the number of accidents; as the amount of unsecured debt increases there will be more casualties.

In a recent year there were more than 115,000 individual insolvencies, including more than 55,000 Individual Voluntary Arrangements (IVAs). The average age of a bankrupt is a person in their forties.. More sobering is the fact that many divorces cite tensions concerning finances as a factor in the breakdown of the relationship. For many, the more accurate marriage vow would have been 'till debt do us part'. Such financial tension exists largely because consumers believe the 'gospel' of buy it because you deserve it' or, 'buy now and pay later with easy monthly payments'. We all know that nothing about those monthly payments is easy.

> *Just as the rich rule the poor, so the borrower is servant to the lender. Proverbs 22:7.*

In an endeavour to win business, some advertise, 'Buy now, no repayments for two (or more) years!' There are a myriad of schemes designed to encourage you to buy 'stuff', that does not have to be paid for today. I received a letter from my car manufacturer advising that the warranty was about to expire. For £900 I could renew my warranty for two years. I was, of course, encouraged to pay this monthly. I visited the local main dealer and was told that their cost was only £576, and I could pay this monthly over three years. At which point Simon, my youngest son, pointed out that if I paid for the warranty in this manner I would end up making three years' payments each month – one of which would be for a lapsed warranty payment of £16 a month for three years and the cover was only for two years. I will revisit the end of this story later in the book.

Watch the adverts and it won't be long before you find an offer for finance. The focus is usually on how you can solve your problems or have what you want by taking up a loan. They make it sound so easy.

Offers for household goods such as suites are often accompanied by reference to 'easy payments'. The actual cost of the item is not mentioned – all that matters is the 'easy' cost **per month**.

Is it important to free yourself from debt so that you can celebrate being debt free? How important is it to take action so that you can freely plan your finances the way that God intends?

WHAT DOES DEBT REALLY COST?

We need to recognise the true cost of debt. Let us consider two types of debt and see the true cost of credit card interest:

CREDIT CARD DEBT

Please study the following table. This seeks to highlight the alarming cost of owing money to card companies and contrasts this with the meagre returns for those saving. Charging an interest rate of 18 per cent on a constant card debt of **£5,555** the interest cost is **£1,000** a year.

The table contrasts what the **lender earns** from that **£1,000** interest a year with their 18 per cent return and contrasts what the **saver earns** at 3 per cent when saving £1,000 a year. There is a difference and it is larger than perhaps you would think! The chart seeks to show the impact over periods up to 40 years.

Amount of interest you would have paid **at the end of each year** on a constant card debt of £5,555 with an interest rate of 18 per cent					
Year 1	Year 10	Year 20	Year 30	Year 40
£1,000	£10,000	£20,000	£30,000	£40,000

BOUGHT

The credit company invests that interest and achieves a return of 18 per cent. Their return on 18 per cent on that £1,000 is:				
Year 1	Year 10	Year 20	Year 30	Year 40
£90	£15,756	£140,557	£836,082	£4,518,685

When the saver invests £1,000 a year and achieves a return of 3 per cent the gain is very different:				
£16	£1,649	£7,304	£18,344	£36,619

How much more does the credit card company earn on that same £1,000? The chart expresses this in multiples:				
6x	9x	19x	45x	123x

Calculator used: thecalculatorsite.com assuming monthly amounts of £83.33 (£1000 p.a.)

HOME MORTGAGE

A 25-year home mortgage, at an annual interest rate of 5% on a repayment basis to the mortgage will require you to pay more than 75 per cent more than the amount originally borrowed.

Original mortgage amount	£120,000
Monthly mortgage payment at 5 per cent (APR-5.12%)	£702
Months paid	300 (25 years)
Total paid	£210,529
Total interest paid	£90,529
Interest cost compared to the original loan	75%

Debt can also extract a physical toll. It often increases stress, which contributes to mental, physical and emotional fatigue. It can stifle creativity and harm relationships. Many people raise their standard of living through debt, only to discover that the burden of debt controls their lifestyles. The car sticker that reads "I owe, I owe, it's off to work I go," is an unfortunate reality for too many people.

WHAT DOES SCRIPTURE SAY ABOUT DEBT?

Scripture's perspective on debt is clear. Read the first portion of Romans 13:8 carefully from several different Bible translations: "Let no debt remain outstanding" (NIV). "Owe nothing to anyone" (NLT). "Keep out of debt and owe no man anything" (AMP).

In Proverbs 22:7 we are reminded why God speaks so directly about debt: "The rich rule over the poor, and the borrower is slave to the lender." When we are in debt, we are in a position of servitude to the lender. Indeed, the deeper we are in debt, the more of a servant we become. We do not have full freedom or discretion to decide where to spend our income because we have legally obligated ourselves to meet these debts.

In 1 Corinthians 7:23 Paul writes, "you were bought at a price; do not become slaves of men." Our Father made the ultimate sacrifice by giving His Son, the Lord Jesus Christ, to die for us. We were truly bought. He now wants His children free to serve Him in whatever way He chooses.

God allowed His Son to die for our sins that we might be free – but Satan seeks to trap us and remove that freedom.

DEBT IS CONSIDERED A CURSE IN THE OLD TESTAMENT

In the Old Testament, one of the rewards for obedience was being out of debt. "If you fully obey the Lord your God and carefully follow all his commands that I give you today, the Lord your God will set you high above all the nations on earth.

All these blessings will come upon you and accompany you... if you obey the Lord your God...if you obey the Lord your God... you will lend to many nations but will borrow from none" (Deuteronomy 28:1-2, 12).

Conversely, indebtedness was one of the curses inflicted for disobedience. "However, if you do not obey the Lord your God and do not carefully follow all his commands and decrees I am giving you today, all these curses will come upon you and overtake you.... The alien who lives among you will rise above you higher and higher, but you will sink lower and lower. He will lend to you, but you will not lend to him. He will be the head, but you will be the tail" (Deuteronomy 28:15, 43-44).

Many of those in debt today might similarly regard debt as a curse that has come upon them.

DEBTS CAN BE CANCELLED AND FORGIVEN

Deuteronomy tells us that God's provision and a faithful, obedient people should mean that there are no poor in the land (Deuteronomy 15:4-5). But the same passage recognises that there will always be poor in the land (verse 11) and there are two implications. Firstly, the people are instructed to lend freely to their neighbour (Deuteronomy 15:8) and this generosity in allowing others to borrow is a source of God's blessing. Secondly, every seven years all debts were to be cancelled (Deuteronomy 15:1-3) and that it was a selfish thought not to lend just before the cancellation of debts (verse 8). What can we learn? However trapped in debt we may be, there is always hope. In our modern context this text does not permit people to borrow with no intent to repay. Nor, in principle, does it permit creditors to pursue repayments from those who cannot repay.

DEBT PRESUMES UPON TOMORROW

When we get into debt, we assume we will earn enough or will have sufficient resources to pay the debt. We plan for our job to continue or our business or investments to be profitable. Scripture cautions us against presumption: "Now listen, you who say, 'Today or tomorrow we will go to this or that city, spend a year there, carry on business and make money'. Why, you do not even know what will happen tomorrow. What is your life? You are a mist that appears for a little while and then vanishes. Instead, you ought to say, 'If it is the Lord's will, we will live and do this or that'" (James 4:13-15).

DEBT MAY DENY US AN OPPORTUNITY TO RECEIVE FROM GOD

The Bible has many warnings about the dangers of debt, but it never says that borrowing money violates God's commandments. It may, however, be unwise to do so.

When we use credit card debt as a quick solution, we effectively deny ourselves the opportunity to let God meet our needs. Moreover, credit card debt is very expensive.

There was a young man who wanted to go to Bible school to become a missionary. He had no money and thought the only way he could afford Bible school was to secure a student loan. However, this would have encumbered him with thousands of pounds of debt by the time he graduated. This would have been an impossible situation. He could not pay back his loan on a missionary's salary.

After a great deal of prayer, he decided to enrol without the help of a student loan and to trust the Lord to meet his needs. He graduated without borrowing anything and grew in his appreciation for how the sovereign, living God could creatively provide for his needs. This was the most valuable lesson learned in Bible school. It prepared him for the mission field where he repeatedly depended on the Lord to meet his needs. Borrowing may deny you an opportunity to demonstrate His faithfulness and provision for your needs.

WHEN CAN WE OWE MONEY?

Financial choices and predicaments are always symptomatic of other issues. Some of the more common issues that lead to credit card debt include a lack of contentment, a lack of self-discipline, the search for security, and sometimes the search for significance.

The bottom line is that we should avoid putting a lender in the place of God by depending on them to meet our needs, and we should not 'play God' in our own lives by deciding that the only way to meet our needs is to borrow.

Scripture is silent on the subject of when we can owe money, but it offers us warnings. The ministry of Your Money Counts considers there are a few areas where debt might be viewed as 'acceptable'.

This 'acceptable debt' is permissible, we believe, only if the following four criteria are met:

1. The item purchased is an asset with the potential to appreciate or to produce an income. That could include house purchase; (more on this very shortly)

2. The value of the item equals or exceeds the amount owed against it

3. The debt is not so large that repayment puts undue strain on your finances

4. The debt does not cause anxiety (Isaiah 32:17).

Practically, that could include investment in a business – making sure that good advice is taken and that plans are realistically formulated. It could also include vocational training.

Let me give you an example of how a home mortgage might qualify. Historically, the home has usually been an appreciating asset – therefore, it meets the first criterion.

Second, if you invest a reasonable deposit you could expect to sell the home for at least enough to repay the mortgage, and this meets the second requirement. Third, the monthly mortgage repayment should not strain your finances. If you meet all the criteria and assume debt, I hope you will immediately establish a goal to repay as quickly as practicable. We cannot be certain that the housing market will appreciate or even maintain current values. Moreover, the loss of a job can interrupt your income. Therefore, I urge you to consider prayerfully paying off all non mortgage debt and not extending the length of a mortgage should you move and buy a new house.

STUDENT DEBT?

There are over three million people who owe student debt. Student debt poses a specific problem and is one that students must address, with or without parental assistance. For most, student debt is almost inevitable for those wishing to obtain a degree. In fact student debt is a particular type of debt. You will never secure another loan at such a low rate of interest, nor one for which the repayments are directly linked to earnings. That said, it is still a burden of debt on people at the start of their adult lives. There is the danger that it creates in young people a culture of debt.

When Simon, our son, was planning to leave school he decided to go to a local university and live at home. We paid for his food and made no charge for rent. During the first two years he worked at a local petrol station and used the income to cover his personal costs. He tithed and saved 20% of his income. During his placement year he earned well and paid a small rent into the household budget. He also earned some part-time income from designing and photography so that by the end of university he had saved £10,000 and had no student debt. With student debt at the time averaging £13,000, that seemed to be a positive £23,000 variance.

Now not for a moment am I suggesting everyone can do this. Not every family can support a student at home, for a variety of reasons. Not every student is able to work, while for many going away from home is part of the university experience. What is important is that students take a mature attitude to student debt, they plan and live within their means, keeping debt to a minimum. On leaving higher education the repayment of student debt should be a priority over seeking an ever higher standard of living.

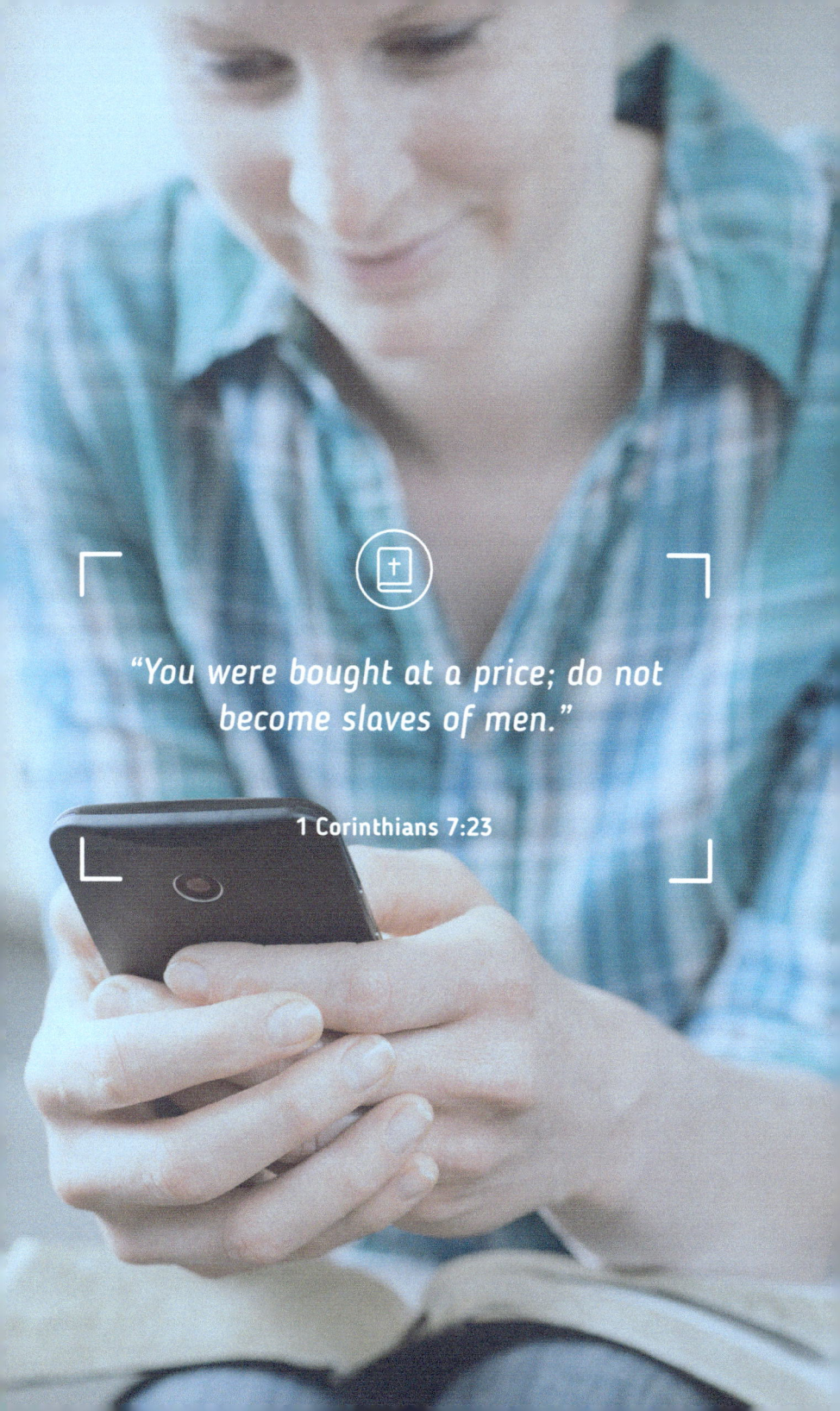

"You were bought at a price; do not become slaves of men."

1 Corinthians 7:23

Getting out of Debt

If you are in debt and you have made a conscious decision to get out of debt, then God's Word will give you the understanding and the godly inspiration to achieve that objective. Your debt free day is now marked clearly on the calendar – even if that might be some way off.

You might have tried to reduce debt and failed. You may need to find someone you trust to help you on this journey. Your prayer and study life may also need to increase as you seek the Lord's guidance. Your determination to become debt free is growing.

THE JOURNEY TO BECOME DEBT FREE

Sadly, many people today are retiring with mortgages and credit cards outstanding and other debts still to be paid off and very little savings. A lifetime in debt. Is it possible to be debt-free? Emphatically, YES!

You should prayerfully make a major financial goal to work toward becoming debt free.

So, you may have tried and failed. What is going to help you solve the debt problem this time? The fact is that now you are going to apply your faith to the plan. You are going to take hold of the Word of the Lord and apply what you know in your heart is God's best for your life.

You may have had help in the past and failed – but not this time.

It is possible that you may have only recently become aware of the amount of your debt – be assured, you are not the first.

You might have leaned a little too heavily on others and perhaps in the end they have let you down – but God will never let you down. With God we know that all things are possible.

So, align your thinking with the Word of the Lord, not **Bought** or any other book although it is good to seek wise counsel – but more about that later.

But before we continue...

Some of the typical questions that come up when I meet people who wish to discuss money, possessions and the Word of God:

Q: "The Bible is only ever negative about debt but those who buy their home almost inevitably have to take out a mortgage and incur long-term debt. How do you square that circle?"

It is a good question that I have been asked on a number of occasions. I know one person who was so convinced that he should not have a mortgage that he sold his house and changed it for a rental property instead. Interestingly, the rent was about 25 per cent more than the cost of the mortgage. I indicated to him that I did not see this as a command in the Bible – but that was his personal decision and one with which he and his wife were very happy. However, over the course of a year he was obligated to pay 12 monthly rental payments – just as he would have done if he had kept the mortgage. So, I do not see the mortgage debt differently from the rent debt. They are both due for payment each month. Debt arises when that obligation is not fully met.

However, my practical solution and guide on this matter has always been consistent regarding mortgages:

Never take a mortgage out unless you are satisfied you could continue to comfortably make the monthly repayments should interest rates increase by two per cent.

When you move home never increase the term. If you started with a 25 year mortgage make sure that it will never go beyond with a mortgage that has more years outstanding than the old mortgage. In fact, why not reduce the term by perhaps two years?

Be very wary of equity release – taking the equity out of the home to maybe pay for an extension, a car or even a holiday. The long-term costs will make that spend far greater than you could imagine. Do not be caught by just considering the additional monthly cost.

Because of your particular circumstances, your path for getting out of debt will be unique to you.

This is going to be a Holy Spirit inspired plan and one that requires perseverance and commitment. Your faith is going to be an important component going forward. And, should you stumble at some point, you are going to recommit knowing that God loves you and is alongside you. We are all weak and earthen vessels and fail at some point, but you are now determined to do this God's way.

In 2 Kings 4:1–7 a widow was threatened with losing her children to her creditor and she appealed to Elisha for help. Elisha instructed the widow to borrow many empty jars from her neighbours. The Lord supernaturally multiplied her meagre resource, a small quantity of oil, and as a result all the jars were filled. She sold the oil and paid her debts to free her children. The same God who provided supernaturally for the widow is interested in you becoming free of debt as well.

The following steps are a guide for your journey. The steps are simple, but following them requires hard work. The goal is Debt Free Day – debtless day, the day when you become absolutely free of debt. I have listed them in what I regard as a hierarchy of importance.

1. PRAY

The first step is the most important. Pray. Ask for the Lord's help and guidance in your journey toward Debt Free Day. He might act immediately, as in the case of the widow, or slowly over time. In either case, prayer is essential.

> *As people begin to eliminate debt and accelerate debt repayment, the Lord blesses their faithfulness. Even if you can afford only a small monthly additional payment to reduce your debt, please do it. The Lord can multiply your efforts.*

2. ACCUMULATE NO NEW DEBT

This is where you have to say to yourself over and over again: "not one penny more". You have been accumulating debt and now you have to stop.

The only way I know to accumulate no additional debt is to pay for everything with cash, a cheque or a debit card at the time of purchase. I do not believe that credit cards are inherently sinful, but they are dangerous. Statistics show that people spend about one-third more when they use credit cards than when they use cash, because they feel they are not really spending money since they are using a plastic card. As one shopper said to another, "I like credit cards a lot more than money because they go so much further!"

Before Rhoda my wife and I became intentional about managing money God's way we had credit and store cards, which in the case of the latter were all at their maximum limit. Today we use cards to serve us, not vice versa. Our card balances are automatically paid monthly by direct debit.

Even though our son manages his finances well, he has twice suffered a penalty for late payment of a card repayment. When I reminded him that our cards were automatically paid off every month he replied that he had not been told he could set up that arrangement. At that point I reminded him that this is a bit of a game the credit card companies play, it is how they make money. Remember they make up the rules so they win – not you!

When I analyse the financial situation of people in debt, I use a simple rule of thumb to determine whether credit cards are too dangerous for them. If they do not pay the entire balance due within two months, I encourage them to perform plastic surgery. Any good scissors will do! When teaching, I usually have a pair of scissors in my pocket; it is amazing how people enjoy having their cards cut up.

If you have a number of credit cards, pay the highest interest card off first. When that card is paid off, use the monthly payment from that card to add to the next credit card payment so reducing the outstanding time and therefore interest payments

3. ESTABLISH A WRITTEN SPENDING PLAN

It is amazing how many people don't have a spending plan – or have one they ignore. The challenge with a spending plan is that it is the starting point of financial discipline, the beginning of a new commitment to plan how you are going to spend less than your income.

In my experience, few people in debt have been using a balanced spending plan where expenditure is more than income. They may have had one neatly filed away in a drawer, but they have not been using it. A spending plan helps you plan ahead and analyse your spending patterns to discover where you can minimise outgoings. It is an effective bridle on impulse spending.

But having a spending plan is only the starting point – monitoring your expenditure, comparing to the plan and working out how your spending habits need to change is mission-critical.

This is almost certain to be a battleground. There are family and household pressures, as well as enticements to spend, spend, spend, promoted by adverts wherever you turn.

But remember, you are going to be strong, no matter what. You are going to overcome. Your finances will come back into shape, and that debt will start to shrink. You are going to be in control of your finances and not all those people who keep chasing you. Except they will chase you to borrow more money. Be wary and always on your guard because as Matthew says: "watch and pray so that you will not fall into temptation. The spirit is willing, but the flesh is weak" (Matthew 26:41).

Balancing the spending plan – there are only four ways to do this:

1. Earn more

2. Spend less

3. Sell possessions, and

4. Be content with what you have.

The world wants to make you discont with the way you look and what possessions you need to lead the 'good life'. If you have children you will know all about the latest craze sweeping around the school. And your children keep pestering you because they don't want to be left behind or the odd ones out. Peer pressure starts at school and it doesn't end there. We live in a culture with an advertising industry that has devised powerful, sophisticated methods of persuading the consumer to buy. Billions will be spent on all forms of advertising in the UK in the next year, including TV, newspapers, billboards, radio, online, and on mobiles and tablets. The people employed in the advertising industry know how to make people buy – that's their job and what they are trained to do. I once attended Disney University in Orlando and was asked, "When inside the park, who do you think Disney is marketing to?" Their answer is 'the children'. Disney does this through creating memories – they even help you frame your photographs in Main Street with their coloured pavements and roads so there is an array of colour in your pictures. Does it work? Well, take my own family and the answer is 'yes'. We took our family to Disney when they were all young and they can still fondly recall the rides and experiences of those holidays. Now married, my daughter took her husband who had never been to a Disney park, together with their two year old daughter – and they returned with lots of memories and pictures.

Another purpose of advertising is to create desires. The marketing profession knows how to create desires and to heighten our inner wants until they become irresistible perceived needs. We do not have to conform to the ways of this world. When we do, how are we able to be transformed by the renewing of our minds? Frequently the message is intended to create discontentment with what we have, or to create desires for things to satisfy.

Interesting but true:

- The more television advertisements you watch, the more you spend
- The more you look at the internet, catalogues and magazines, the more you spend
- The more you shop, the more you spend.

Again, our family is again evidence of this. When my daughter suddenly wanted a special box of Disney characters, I knew she had seen a television commercial. Careful choice of our television habits and viewing also limits our wants.

4. LIST YOUR ASSETS – SELL WHAT YOU ARE NOT USING

List every possession you own: your home, car, furniture, etc. Evaluate the complete list to determine whether you should sell any assets.

It is surprising how attitudes and perspectives can change when going through this exercise. I have known people who have sold a car, uploaded unwanted items onto a website for sale or to give away. Your attitude toward things will determine your success in working your way out of debt. Don't think about how much you will lose or what you paid for the item you are selling. Think about how much you will gain so that you can reduce your debt immediately.

Statistics show that people spend about one-third more when they use credit cards than when they use cash, because they feel they are not really spending money since they are using a plastic card.

5. LIST YOUR LIABILITIES – EVERYTHING YOU OWE

Many people, particularly if they owe a lot of money, do not know exactly what they owe. However, you must list your debts to get an accurate picture of your current financial situation. You also need to list the interest rate your creditors are charging for each debt.

	Amount Owed	Monthly Payment	Interest Rate
Mortgage			
Credit cards			
Bank overdraft			
Loans			
Student loans			
Loans from relatives			
Hire purchase, leasing etc.			
Business loans			
Others e.g. catalogues			
Total debts			

Please visit Yourmoneycounts.org for a full debt list spreadsheet.

DEBT LIST – WHAT IS OWED?

If you use spreadsheets, create one with your debts listed in a column and then use the rows for months so that you have a worksheet similar to the table above, but extended to show each month's repayment and the overall repayment. This spreadsheet will give you a plan to follow. Often, seeing a debt reduction plan gives hope and provides a powerful motivation to implement the plan. If you are experienced in using spreadsheets, then you could set up a number of interlinking ones with your income and expenditure and cash flows using the 'special paste' functionality, and prepare a plan that would impress any accountant!

As you analyse the interest rates on your debt list, you will discover that credit costs vary greatly. Listing your debts will help you establish a priority of debt reduction.

6. THE ORDER OF REPAYING YOUR DEBTS – TWO APPROACHES:

1. DEBT STACKING

The 'debt stacking' method recommends that you make a list of all your debts, ranked by interest rate, from highest to lowest.

Pros: This method saves you the most money in interest payments.

Cons: It might take a long time to get a high-balance debt crossed off your list. You may feel frustrated after investing so much time and energy towards paying down a loan, without feeling the mental 'victory' of crossing it off your list.

2. THE SNOWBALL STRATEGY

How do you 'snowball' yourself out of debt?

Pay off your smallest credit card debt.

Review your credit card debts. In addition to making the minimum payments on all your cards, focus on accelerating the payment of your smallest high-interest credit card first. You will be encouraged as you make progress, finally eliminating that debt.

After you pay off the first credit card, apply what you were used to pay toward the next smallest one.

After the second card is paid off, apply what you were paying on the first and second toward the third smallest credit card, and so forth. That's the snowball strategy in action!

Pay off your smallest consumer debt.

After you have paid off all your credit cards, focus on paying off your consumer debts in exactly the same way as you wiped out your card debt. Make the minimum payments on any of your store card debts, but focus on accelerating the payment of your smallest higher-interest store card debt first. Then, after you pay off the first store card debt, apply its payment toward the next smallest one. After the second one is paid off, apply what you were paying on the first and second to pay off the third, and so forth until you have repaid your credit card and store card debts and then you can start on repaying your unsecured and other debts.

WHICH METHOD SHOULD YOU USE?

Paying off debt is a little like dieting. Sure, there are more 'ideal' eating plans out there, but let's be realistic: most people aren't going to stick to a perfect diet. The 'best' diet is the one that you'll adhere to.

7. CAN YOU EARN MORE?

Many people hold jobs that simply do not produce enough income to meet their outgoings. Furthermore, where income might have been adequate yesterday that may not be the case if your expenses are above your income. Two issues are important regarding earning additional income. First, decide in advance to pay off debts with the increased earnings. We tend to spend more than we make, whether we earn much or little. Spending always seems to keep ahead of earning. Second, earn additional income without harming your relationship with the Lord or with your loved ones. Be creative in looking for jobs and balance the additional income against other factors such as caring for elderly parents or young children and not taking on so much that you wear yourself out or have no time left to share with your partner.

These are only some of the many ways to to get out of debt more quickly. However, no matter how much additional income you earn, the key is a commitment that the money is applied to reduce the debt and not to a higher level of spending.

8. CONSIDER A RADICAL CHANGE IN YOUR LIFESTYLE

A growing number of people have lowered their expenses significantly to get out of debt more quickly. In order to achieve this some have sold their homes and moved to smaller ones, rented apartments or moved in with family members. Others have sold cars with large monthly payments and have purchased inexpensive used cars for cash. They have temporarily lowered their cost of living to become free from debt.

9. DO NOT GIVE UP!

Recognise from the beginning there will be a hundred reasons why you should quit or delay your efforts to get out of debt. Don't yield to the temptation of not following through on your commitment. Don't stop until you have reached the marvellous goal of debt-free living. Remember, getting out of debt is just plain hard work, but the freedom is worth the struggle.

HOW DO WE ESCAPE THE CAR DEBT TRAP?

Car debt is one of the leading causes of consumer indebtedness. A large proportion of the cars on the road today are financed. The average change cycle for a car is between two and three years. A new car lasts on average at least 10 years.

Here is how you can escape the car debt trap.

1. First, decide in advance to keep your car for at least six years.

2. Second, continue with the payments until the agreement has been fulfilled.

3. Third, continue paying the monthly car payment but into your own savings account. Then, when you are ready to replace your car, the saved cash plus the part exchange value should be sufficient to buy a good, low-mileage used car without going into debt.

4. Resist any car-financing plan that has a built in mechanism that requires you to make a 'balloon' payment at the end of the period of the car 'purchase' contract. The payments on that new car might well be low and affordable but you may well be caught having to sell or return the car for another new car. Caught in the car debt trap!

INVESTMENT DEBT

I have a friend who recently admitted that he was deep in debt as a result of borrowing money with the intention to invest in some leading FTSE shares whose share price had fallen dramatically. However, he was persuaded to redirect his investment into a commodity company. The result? Sadly, very sadly, he lost all of his money in the commodity company which went into liquidation. The company he had intended to invest in recovered and he would have made a 900 per cent profit. He has spent over 10 years trying to repay the debt which still partly remains outstanding.

Should you borrow money to make an investment? I believe it is permissible, but only if you are not personally required to guarantee the repayment of the debt. The investment for which you borrow and any money invested should be the sole collateral for the debt.

There is the possibility of difficult or catastrophic financial events over which you have no control. It is painful to lose your investment, but it is much more serious to jeopardise meeting your needs by risking all your assets on investment debt. This position may appear too conservative; however, many people have lost everything by guaranteeing debt on investments that turned sour. I do not, however, believe it is wise or godly to borrow to speculate (e.g. on stocks and shares).

With all your investment decisions, taking appropriate and qualified advice is essential.

BUSINESS AND CHURCH DEBT

I also want to encourage you to pray about becoming debt-free in your business and church. Many are beginning to pay off all business-related debts, and scores of churches are aggressively working toward satisfying their debts.

Some people delay payments in order to use the creditor's money as long as possible. There are seminars that actually teach people to do just that, but this is not biblical. Proverbs 3:27–28 reads: "do not withhold good from those to whom it is due, when it is in the power of your hand to do so. Do not say to your neighbour 'go, and come back, and tomorrow I will give it,' when you have it with you" (NKJV). Godly people should pay their debts and bills as promptly as they can. We have a policy of trying to pay each personal bill within a week of receiving it, to demonstrate to others that knowing Jesus Christ has made us financially responsible.

SHOULD YOU USE ALL YOUR SAVINGS TO PAY OFF DEBT?

In my opinion it is wise not to deplete all your savings to pay off debt. Maintain a reasonable level of savings to provide for the unexpected. If you apply all your savings against debt and the unexpected does occur, you probably will be forced to incur more debt to meet the need.

BANKRUPTCY

In bankruptcy, a court of law declares a person unable to pay their debts. Depending upon the type of bankruptcy, the court will either allow the debtor to develop a plan to repay the creditors, or the court will distribute the proceeds from the sale of assets among the creditors as payment for the debts.

Should a godly person declare bankruptcy? The answer is that applying for bankruptcy or an Individual Voluntary Arrangement should not be entertained lightly. Psalm 37:21 tells us that "the wicked borrow and do not repay" and this certainly applies to borrowing with no intent or no concerted effort to repay. But the verse cannot possibly rule out debt cancellation when Deuteronomy 15 is considered.

In my opinion bankruptcy is permissible in three circumstances:

- Where a creditor forces a person into bankruptcy
- When the borrower experiences such extreme financial difficulties that there is no option. There are occasions when bankruptcy is the only viable option when the financial challenges become too extreme to reverse. This option needs to be exercised only after all others have been explored, or,
- If the emotional health of the borrower is at stake because of an inability to cope with the pressure of aggressive creditors, bankruptcy can be an option.

For example, if a husband deserts his wife and children, leaving her with business and family debts, but she could then become primarily responsible, and may not have the resources or income to meet those obligations. The emotional trauma of an unwanted divorce, coupled with harassment from unsympathetic creditors, may be too much for her to bear.

After a person goes through bankruptcy, they could seek counsel from a competent debt counselling service provider to determine if it's legally permissible to repay the debt, even though they are not obligated to do so. If it is allowable, they should make every effort to repay the debt. For a large debt, this may be a long-term goal that is largely dependent upon the Lord supernaturally providing the resources.

GUARANTEEING THE DEBT OF OTHERS

The issue of making guarantees is related to debt. A person who guarantees a loan becomes legally responsible for the debt of another. It is just as if you went to the bank, borrowed the money and gave it to your friend or relative who is asking you to act as guarantor.

Research in the US by the Fed-Trade commission reveals that 50 per cent of those who guaranteed bank loans ended up making payments. Seventy-five per cent of those who guaranteed for finance company loans ended up making payments. Unfortunately, few guarantors plan for default. The casualty rate is so high because the professional lender has analysed the loan and concluded "I won't touch this with a 10-foot pole unless I can get someone who is financially responsible to guarantee this loan."

Fortunately, Scripture speaks very clearly about guaranteeing. Proverbs 17:18 reads "it's poor judgement to guarantee another person's debt or put up security for a friend" (NLT). The words 'poor judgement' are better translated 'destitute of mind'.

A parent often acts as a guarantor for their child's first car, but we decided not to. We wanted to model for our children the importance of not guaranteeing, and we also wished to discourage them from using debt. Instead, we trained them to plan ahead and save for the purchase of their car.

If you want to help your children out, give them a gift. Sometimes in the UK it is simply not possible to avoid being guarantor. When the daughter of a friend started college the halls of residence insisted on him acting as guarantor as a condition of allocating his daughter a room.

In these situations you must put the money aside or perhaps expect a default. You may see this as your children transitioning from being provided for at home to being responsible for their own housing costs.

Use sound judgement and never guarantee a liability or become surety for any debt unless, as above, a guarantee is mandatory. If you have guaranteed, Scripture gives you very direct counsel. Proverbs reads: "My child, if you have put up security for a friend's debt or agreed to guarantee the debt of a stranger – if you have trapped yourself by your agreement and are caught by what you said – follow my advice and save yourself, for you have placed yourself at your friend's mercy. Now swallow your pride; go and beg to have your name erased. Don't put it off; do it now! Don't rest until you do. Save yourself like a gazelle escaping from a hunter, like a bird fleeing from a net" (Proverbs 6:1–5, NLT).

Counsel – seeking Godly wisdom

When it comes to finance there are options for you to consider. Some counselling services are run by Christians and others by independent organisations that have no overt Christian foundations. They all desire to help.

Louise and Jeremy were faced with an uncomfortable decision. Louise's brother and his wife had just moved to Bristol from Surrey. Because they had experienced financial difficulties and been through an Independent Voluntary Arrangement, the bank would not lend them the necessary funds for the mortgage unless they had someone to act as guarantor. They asked Jeremy and Louise to find someone. Louise pleaded with Jeremy to do so; however, he was reluctant.

When they came for advice to resolve this problem, I asked them to read the verses from the Bible that addressed guaranteeing. When Louise read the passages she responded "Who am I to argue with God? We shouldn't act as guarantors." Jeremy was relieved.

Two years later, Louise's brother and his wife were divorced and he was declared bankrupt again. Can you imagine the strain on their marriage if they had guaranteed that debt? They would not have been able to survive financially.

Fortunately, they sought counsel. This is in sharp contrast to our culture's practice that encourages you to be a rugged

> *Two are better than one, because they have a good return for their work. Ecclesiastes 4:9*

individualist who makes decisions alone and unafraid, coping with any financial pressure in stoical silence.

King Solomon dominated the world scene in his time. Known as the first great commercial king of Israel, he was a skilled diplomat and director of extensive building, shipping and mining ventures. However, Solomon is most often remembered as the wisest king who ever lived. In fact, he made wisdom a subject of study. In Proverbs he wrote: "wisdom is more precious than rubies, and nothing you desire can compare with her" (8:11). Solomon's practical recommendations for embracing wisdom are also found in Proverbs: "Get all the advice and instruction you can, so you will be wise the rest of your life" (19:20, NLT). And, "The way of a fool seems right to him, but a wise man listens to advice" (12:15).

FROM WHOM SHOULD WE SEEK COUNSEL?

The Bible directs us toward several sources of good counsel:

SCRIPTURE

The psalmist wrote "your laws please me; they give me wise advice" (Psalm 119:24, NLT). Moreover, the Bible makes this remarkable claim about itself: "For the word of God is living and active. Sharper than any double-edged sword...it judges the thoughts and attitudes of the heart" (Hebrews 4:12). I have found this to be true. The Bible is a living book that our Lord uses to communicate His direction and truths to all generations. It is the first filter through which we should put our financial decisions. If the Scriptures clearly answer our question, we do not have to go any further because it contains the Lord's written, revealed will. If the Bible is not specific about a particular issue, we should subject our decision to the second source of counsel: godly people.

GODLY PEOPLE

"The mouth of the righteous man utters wisdom, and his tongue speaks what is just. The law of his God is in his heart; his feet do not slip" (Psalm 37:30–31). The apostle Paul recognised the benefit of godly counsel. After he was converted on the Damascus road, he was never alone in his public ministry. He knew and appreciated the value of a couple of extra sets of eyes looking down that straight and narrow road. Timothy, Barnabas, Luke or someone else was always with him.

In fact, in the New Testament, 'saint' is never used in the singular. It is always in the plural. Someone has described the Christian life as not one of independence from each other but of dependence upon each other. Nowhere is this more clearly illustrated than in Paul's discussion concerning the body of Christ in the 12th chapter of 1 Corinthians. Each of us is

A person standing alone can be attacked and defeated, but two can stand back-to-back and conquer. Three are even better, for a triple-braided cord is not easily broken. Ecclesiastes 4:12, NLT

pictured as a different part of this body. Our ability to function effectively is dependent upon members working together. In other words, to operate in an optimal way, we need other people to help us. God has given each one of us certain abilities and gifts, but God has not given any one person all the skills they need to be most productive.

1. Spouse. If you are married, your spouse is to be your primary source of human counsel. A husband and wife are one. A husband and wife need each other to achieve the proper balance for a good and wise decision. In many relationships one partner is much better at managing personal finance than the other. It is important for the other partner to recognise this but also to work together in managing personal finances. Regardless of your spouse's business education or financial aptitude you must cultivate and seek their counsel. You may feel that you have the business background or financial skills, but your partner may also have or can develop excellent business and financial skills, and their insight will always enrich your own.

I have known bereaved families whose distress has been accentuated by no-one knowing the state of the finances. One thing of which we are all certain is death, and keeping your spouse involved in home finances is healthy. Normally, there is one spouse who takes the lead responsibility with the other happy to look on. Rhoda and I discuss our expenditure every month, we review the previous month and look at how we fared compared to the spending plan. However, I have also known couples who argue about their finances. Discussing household finances in an open, loving and sensitive way, and allowing both to be involved in decisions, is ultimately an area where the marriage relationship should be made to work well.

Tried it before and it didn't work? Try again, don't give up. One of you might take responsibility for preparing the end of month numbers; let the other person see the numbers and then get together to discuss them. Rhoda and I usually spend about 10 minutes going through our finances every month.

Seeking the counsel of your spouse also helps preserve your relationship because you will both experience the consequences of a decision. If you both agree about a decision, even if it proves to be disastrous, your relationship is more likely to remain intact than become fractious as a result of an issue concerning finances.

2. Parents. My children have all at some time come to us for advice. Since my daughter married, she and her husband have approached me once concerning a business opportunity. While I am always there for my children, I do not now expect them to come to me for advice, although they do. We have been blessed with children who have shared their career developments with us.

Proverbs 6:20-22 says: "my son, keep your father's commands and do not forsake your mother's teaching... When you walk, they will guide you; when you sleep, they will watch over you; when you awake, they will speak to you."

It is not uncommon for an unspoken barrier to be erected between a child and their parents. Asking for advice is a way to honour them and to build a bridge across any wall.

A word of caution from God's word: Genesis 2:24 reads: "for this reason a man will leave his father and mother and be united to his wife, and they will become one flesh." Although a husband and wife may seek the counsel of their parents, the advice of the parents should be subordinate to the advice of a spouse.

THE LORD

During the process of searching the Bible and obtaining the counsel of godly people, we need to seek direction from the Lord and His Word. In Isaiah 9:6 we are told that one of the Lord's names is 'Wonderful Counsellor'. The Psalms clearly identify the Lord as our counsellor. "I [The Lord] will instruct you and teach you in the way you should go; I will counsel you and watch over you" (Psalm 32:8). "I will praise the Lord, who counsels me" (Psalm 16:7).

We receive the counsel of the Lord by praying and listening. Tell the Lord about your concerns and need for specific direction. Then quietly listen for His still, small voice.

A MULTITUDE OF COUNSELLORS

The Bible encourages us to obtain advice from a multitude of counsellors. Proverbs 15:22 tells us "plans fail for lack of counsel, but with many advisers they succeed." And Proverbs 11:14 says, "where there is no counsel, the people fall; but in the multitude of counsellors there is safety" (NKJV).

The older I have become the more I recognise my need for a multitude of counsellors. Each of us has a limited range of knowledge and experience, and we need others, with their own unique backgrounds, to give us insights and alternatives we might not consider without their advice. We should find those who are wise as well as seeking to gain wisdom and understanding ourselves. Surrounding yourself with those who are wise can benefit your financial decisions while also significantly contributing to your emotional and spiritual health. Most people need support and encouragement at some time in their lives.

Rhoda and I have learned that when someone is subjected to a painful circumstance, it is not necessarily easy for them to make wise, objective decisions. We have known those who have experienced the safety of having a group of people around them on whose counsel they can depend. It is not always easy to receive counsel, and sometimes that counsel can be rejected – especially if it hurts. I am more receptive to constructive criticism when it comes from someone I respect, someone who really does have my best interests at heart. Solomon describes the benefits of dependence upon one another in this passage:

"Two are better than one, because they have a good reward for their labour. For if they fall, one will lift up his companion.

But woe to him who is alone when he falls, for he has no one to help him up…. Though one may be overpowered by another, two can withstand him. And a threefold cord is not quickly broken" (Ecclesiastes 4:9-12 NKJV).

BIG DECISIONS

Because of their importance and permanence, some decisions deserve more attention than others. Decisions concerning a career or a house purchase, for example, affect us for a longer period of time than most other choices we make. Throughout Scripture we are instructed to wait upon the Lord. Whenever you face a major decision or experience a sense of confusion concerning a course of action, I encourage you to set aside some time to pray, fast and listen quietly for His will.

COUNSEL TO AVOID

We need to avoid one particular source of counsel. "Blessed is the man who does not walk in the counsel of the wicked" (Psalm 1:1). The word 'blessed' literally means 'happy many times over'. The word 'wicked' is a strong word and is often used to describe people who behave in an extremely cruel manner. However, the dictionary widens the use of the term to include those who are sinful or iniquitous, while the first three synonyms on dictionary.com are unrighteous, ungodly and godless.

There are people who would advise us to do things that are wrong or would take advantage of us in financial matters for their advantage. We need discernment. If anything sounds too good to be true, it probably is!

In my opinion, if there is no suitably qualified Christian, then technical or professional advice should be sought from those you, or maybe someone whose counsel you trust, deem qualified to advise. Armed with that advice, your financial decision should be based on prayer and possibly a second opinion from those who know the Lord.

NEVER, NEVER, NEVER SEEK THE COUNSEL OF FORTUNE TELLERS OR MEDIUMS

The Bible bluntly tells us never to seek the advice of fortune tellers, mediums or spiritualists: "Do not turn to mediums or seek out spiritualists, for you will be defiled by them. I am the Lord your God" (Leviticus 19:31). Study this next passage carefully: "Saul died because he was unfaithful to the Lord... and even consulted a medium for guidance, and did not enquire of the Lord. So the Lord put him to death" (1 Chronicles 10:13 – 14).

Saul died, in part, because he went to a medium. We should be sure to avoid any methods they use in forecasting the future, such as horoscopes, ouija boards, tarot cards and all other practices of the occult.

BE CAREFUL OF THOSE WHO ARE BIASED

We need to be cautious of the counsel of biased people. When receiving financial advice, ask yourself this question: What stake does this person have in the outcome of my decision? If the adviser will profit, always seek a second, unbiased opinion.

"I will instruct you and teach you in the way you should go; I will counsel you and watch over you."

Psalm 32:8

Consider this

Free to serve Him

GET MORE INSIGHTS AT
→ WWW.YOURMONEYCOUNTS.ORG.UK

If in debt do all you can not to go one penny further in debt. Incurring debt has to come to an end.

Schedule all your debts and develop a debt repayment plan. Be intentional and determined.

If you have car debt – make sure this is the last time you borrow money on a car.

Do not stand as guarantor for others.

Seek good godly counsel.

Key Questions

What has stopped you succeeding with downsizing debt that will not hold you back again?

What do you need to do to get to grips with debt repayment?

What immediate steps can you take?

What level of short term savings do you need?

Do you need to seek counsel and if so who will you ask that you can trust and has what it takes to be of help?

4

Growing in generosity

Giving | Tithing

There is one very clear difference between the world's approach to finances and God's. That is intentional generosity. Giving is a godly command. It helps us outwork God's plan that our faith should not be in our bank balance but in Him. The act of giving is one way that we tell ourselves we have enough. Giving is not God's way of raising money. It's God's way of raising people into the likeness of His Son.

In looking at generosity it is important to remember that God owns everything, and it is more blessed to give than to receive.

Giving

There are more verses related to giving than any other money-related issue. There are many commands, practical suggestions, examples and exhortations concerning this facet of stewardship. Throughout the Bible, covetousness and greed are condemned, while generosity and charity are encouraged.

THE RIGHT ATTITUDE IN GIVING

Giving with the proper attitude is crucial. Paul writes in 1 Corinthians 13:3, "If I give all I possess to the poor...but have not love, I gain nothing." It is hard to imagine anything more commendable than giving everything to the poor. But if it is done with the wrong attitude, without love, it is of no gain to the giver. The Lord sets the example of giving motivated by love. "For God so loved the world that He gave his one and only Son" (John 3:16). Note the sequence: because God loved, He gave.

If giving is simply giving to our church, to a ministry, a charitable organisation or to a needy person, it is charity and that is no bad thing in itself. But when our giving is first to the Lord it becomes an act of worship. Because Jesus Christ is our Creator, our Saviour and our faithful Provider, we can express our gratefulness and love by giving our gifts to Him.

Of course, a gift benefits the recipient, but according to God's economy, if a gift is given with the proper attitude, the giver benefits more than the receiver. "Remember the words of the Lord Jesus, that He said 'it is more blessed to give than to receive'" (Acts 20:35 NKJV).

Stop and examine yourself. What is your attitude toward giving? I cannot stress too much the importance of giving with the proper attitude.

Above all else, giving directs our attention and heart to Christ. Matthew 6:21 tells us "for where your treasure is, there your heart will be also." This is why it is so necessary to go through the process of consciously giving each gift to the person of Jesus Christ. When you give your gift to Him, your heart will automatically be drawn to the Lord.

Our heavenly Father wants us, as His children, to be conformed to the image of His Son. The character of Christ is unselfish. Unfortunately, humans are by nature selfish. One of the key ways our character becomes conformed to Christ is by habitual giving. Someone once said, "Giving is not God's way of raising money; it is God's way of raising people into the likeness of His Son." John Wesley, based in Bristol for many years, said, "Money never stays with me. It would burn if it did. I throw it out of my hands as soon as possible, lest it should find its way to my heart." The Lord understands that for us

> *You are never more like Jesus than when you are giving.*
> Pastor Johnny Hunt

to develop into the people He wants us to be, we must learn how to share our possessions freely. If we don't, our inbred selfishness will grow and dominate us.

Matthew 6:20 tells us, "but store up for yourselves treasures in heaven, where moth and rust do not destroy, and where thieves do not break in and steal." The Lord tells us that there really is something akin to the 'Royal Bank of Heaven'. He wants us to know that we can invest for eternity.

Paul wrote "not that I am looking for a gift, but I am looking for what may be credited to your account" (Philippians 4:17). A spiritual account exists for each of us in heaven. We will be privileged to enjoy it forever. We 'can't take it with us,' but we can make deposits into our heavenly account before we die.

The Bible is full of God's promises to His faithful children. Rewards both now and forever are in store for those who love and obey Him.

God can choose to bless our giving in this world with increased material possessions. But what if He does not? Most of the verses about eternal rewards do not mention money or possessions as rewards for giving. Instead, they mention rewards in heaven.

Giving with the proper attitude also results in a material increase flowing to the giver. Proverbs 11:24–25 informs us: "one man gives freely, yet gains even more; another withholds unduly, but comes to poverty. A generous man will prosper; he who refreshes others will himself be refreshed."

2 Corinthians 9: 6 and 8 tells us: "Whoever sows sparingly will also reap sparingly, and whoever sows generously will also reap generously. God is able to make all grace abound to you… that you will abound in every good work."

Giving is not the key that unlocks personal prosperity. To give in order to receive contradicts the importance of attitude mentioned earlier.

Remember also that material prosperity was far from the experience both of the Macedonian church that Paul commended to the Corinthians (2 Corinthians 8:1-2) and the Jerusalem church for whom Paul was organising the collection.

Paul himself knew times of hardship alongside plenty and he reminds the church at Corinth that few had social or economic standing when they were called. Of course Jesus himself had few possessions and depended on others for his physical needs. What seems certain is that generosity will never impoverish us either spiritually or financially.

Thomas Gouge, a noted minister in the 1600s, said: "I dare challenge all the world to give me one instance, or at least any considerable number of instances of any truly merciful men, whose charity has undone them. But as living wells the more they are drawn, the more freely they spring and flow; so the substance of liberal men doth oftentimes, if not, ordinarily, multiply in the very distribution: even as the five loaves and few fishes did multiply in their distribution by the hands of the Redeemer. And the widow's oil increased by pouring it out for the holy prophet."

Reverend Gouge personally lived out this testimony as he funded his own ministry as well as many poor people in his area using the estate left by his father.

Secondly, note carefully why the Lord returns an increase materially: "That...you may have an abundance for every good deed." As shown in the diagram on the next page, the Lord produces an increase so that we may give more and have our needs met at the same time.

However, there are also many examples in Scripture of God's current blessings. Much of the reward for giving that was promised in the Old Testament related to increased crops and herds as well as protection from enemies – all of which relate to physical rewards during life on earth.

THE AMOUNT TO GIVE

Under the Law of Moses a tithe, or 10 per cent, of crops was required to be given by all those who grew crops, to support the Levitical priesthood who were to offer sacrifices. When

```
        Giving
       ↗      ↘
  Increase   Needs met
       ↖      ↙
```

the children of Israel disobeyed this commandment, it was regarded as robbing God Himself. Listen to these solemn words in Malachi's days: "Should people cheat God? Yet you have cheated me! But you ask 'What do you mean? When did we ever cheat you?' You have cheated me of the tithes and offerings due to me. You are under a curse, for your whole nation has been cheating me " (Malachi 3:8-9, NLT).

In addition to the tithe of produce, the Hebrews were to give offerings. Furthermore, the Lord made special provisions for the needs of the poor. For example, every seven years all debts were cancelled, and special rules governed harvesting so that the poor could gather food.

In the New Testament the tithe is neither specifically rejected nor specifically recommended. It does teach us to give in proportion to the material blessing we have received, and it especially commends sacrificial giving. In the New Testament all the examples of giving show amounts of much more than 10 per cent.

What I like about the tithe or any fixed percentage of giving is that it is systematic, and the amount of the gift is easy to compute. The danger of the tithe is that it can be treated simply as another bill to be paid. By not giving out of a heart of love, I place myself in a position where I cannot receive the blessings the Lord has designed for a giver. Another potential danger of tithing is the view that once I have tithed, I have fulfilled all my obligations to give.

For Christians the tithe should be the beginning of their giving, not the full extent.

Scripture is unclear on exactly how much we should give. I believe this lack of clarity is because the decision concerning the amount an individual gives should be based on a personal relationship with God. As we seek the guidance of the Spirit through an active prayer life, giving suddenly becomes an exciting adventure.

HOW MUCH SHOULD YOU GIVE?

To answer this question, first submit yourself to God. Earnestly seek His will for you. "And they did do as we expected, but they gave themselves first to the Lord and then to us in keeping with God's will" (2 Corinthians 8:5).

Rhoda and I have given a great deal of thought and prayer to the question of how much we should give. We have concluded that the tithe is the starting point for our giving plan. Then, we give over and above the tithe as we feel led, and as God prospers or directs.

SOWING AND REAPING

The Bible calls this principle "sowing and reaping" and God promises that He will always supply seed to those who sow generously. He will always give us more if we are faithful with what we have already been given. This principle is to encourage us in our giving; it brings a freedom and confidence to our generosity. The principle of sowing and reaping is explained clearly in 2 Corinthians 9:6-11 "Remember this: Whoever sows sparingly will also reap sparingly, and whoever sows generously will also reap generously. Each man should give what he has decided in his heart to give, not reluctantly or under compulsion, for God loves a cheerful giver. And God is able to make all grace abound to you, so that in all things at all times; having all that you need, you will abound in every good work. As it is written: "He has scattered abroad his gifts to the poor; his righteousness endures forever." Now He who supplies seed to the sower and bread for food will also supply and increase your store of seed and will enlarge the harvest of your righteousness. You will be made rich in every way so that you can be generous on every occasion, and through us your generosity will result in thanksgiving to God."

These verses show us that if we give little, we should expect little in return. If we give bountifully though, God will bless us so that we can give even more. The only way we will be able to be greater givers in the future is to begin giving generously now. Our motivation shouldn't be to give so that we can gain, it should be to give so that we can give more. We should strive to be like God who is the greatest giver of all.

God doesn't need our money, He is God. He can and does operate without our help. So why is there so much advice about money in the Bible? What does God want more than our money? He wants our heart to turn to Him.

GIVING STRENGTHENS YOUR FAITH

It is very easy to get caught up thinking that "if I can please God, then..." But when we start thinking in this way we tend to overlook everything that God has already done for us. We try so hard to please God with our works that the hand of God becomes constrained. God doesn't want to reward our works as this is contrary to how we are meant to function. Deuteronomy 8:17-18 highlights this. It says "You may say to yourself, 'My power and the strength of my hands have produced this wealth for me.' But remember the Lord your God, for it is He who gives you the ability to produce wealth, and so confirms his covenant, which he swore to your forefathers, as it is today."

As we give back to God, it helps us to remember, and be grateful for, everything that He has done and continues to do for us. It reminds us that His supply has nothing to do with what we can or cannot do on our own. By choosing to give back to God we are making a tangible decision to have faith in His provision. We are making a choice, a commitment to rely on God and to stop trying to operate in self-sufficiency. After all, He designed us to operate out of relationship with Him, and He wants to be our supplier.

> *And my God will meet all your needs according to his glorious riches in Christ Jesus. Philippians 4:19*

GIVING HELPS US TO LIVE IN GOD'S FREEDOM

When we come to a place where we can rely on God and what He has does for us, it brings with it a sense of freedom; freedom from striving to do things in our own strength, with the futility of our own thinking. Generosity also helps to free us from destructive materialism and greed. We know that money and the possibility of getting more money can sometimes exert a hold over us. Money can be a very powerful motivator, and it is easy to get caught up with going after more. Giving will enable us to live contentedly under the riches of God's blessing - this is the antidote to becoming side-tracked by greed.

"No one can serve two masters. Either he will hate the one and love the other, or he will be devoted to the one and despise the other. You cannot serve both God and Money" (Matthew 6:24).

This sense of freedom doesn't happen when we give unless we act with the right understanding. If we find that we are giving through fear, because we think our salvation is dependent on our giving, then we have misunderstood the biblical design for giving. It is faith in Jesus Christ and His death on the cross that seals our salvation. When we give we need to give voluntarily, as it says in 2 Corinthians 9:7: "Each man should give what he has decided in his heart to give, not reluctantly or under compulsion, for God loves a cheerful giver." Paul then goes on to say in verse 8: "And God is able to make all grace abound to you, so that in all things at all times, having all that you need, you will abound in every good work." We need to give from an understanding that God is our provider, not because we feel forced or coerced.

It is also important to remember that we shouldn't give to earn God's favour, and we shouldn't think that if we give that we are somehow better or holier than someone who doesn't. We are to respect each other's decisions as each decides in his heart what to give. Yes, in as much as failure to do so diminishes our blessing and our potential for effective service and responsible stewardship.

As we have seen we are also instructed in the Bible to give cheerfully (2 Corinthians 9:7), extravagantly (Mark 14:3-9), sacrificially (2 Corinthians 8:2-3) and not for the purpose of earning man's favour (Matthew 6:2). Giving is truly a test of our hearts. It is only possible to tithe and be generous in the manner that God intended when we have a revelation of God's heart towards us, when we realise that there is an open heaven over us. When we tithe and give from the right perspective, we will be blessed of God and because of our right understanding, that blessing will flow through our lives to others and we will begin to fulfil the heart of God.

THE PATTERN OF GIVING

During Paul's third missionary journey he wrote to the churches at Corinth concerning a promised collection to meet the needs of the persecuted believers in Jerusalem. "On the first day of every week, each one of you should set aside a sum of money in keeping with his income, saving it up, so that when I come no collections will have to be made" (1 Corinthians 16:2). His comments provide practical instruction about giving. Let me call this pattern 'Paul's Pod of Ps' – giving that is personal, out of a periodic income, private deposit, premeditated and prayerful.

GIVING SHOULD BE PERSONAL

Giving is the privilege and responsibility of every Christian, young and old, rich and poor.

GIVING SHOULD BE PERIODIC

The Lord understands that we need to give regularly "on the first day of every week." Giving regularly helps draw us consistently to Christ.

GIVING SHOULD BE OUT OF A PRIVATE DEPOSIT

"Put aside and save...." If you experience difficulty in monitoring the money you have decided to give, consider opening a separate bank account. You might also do something as simple as setting aside a special 'giving jar' into which you deposit the money you intend to give. I have a jar into which I throw all my loose change and then sometimes that which is not quite so loose. Every year Rhoda counts it out and gives it away. Yes, I know that my own giving should be in secret – but maybe it is an example I could encourage you to follow.

The most gratifying part of setting aside money has been the thrill of praying that God would make us aware of needs and then enable us to respond.

GIVING SHOULD BE PREMEDITATED

In order to ensure that we give and give generously, I entrust Rhoda with the responsibility of our regular giving. Then, when an opportunity arises we discuss giving from our gifts budget. She enjoys doing all the administration and I am blessed as our God-given privilege of giving is not thwarted by the warring of the flesh.

The supreme example of premeditated giving was set by our Saviour: "who for the joy set before Him endured the cross" (Hebrews 12:2).

TO WHOM DO WE GIVE?

We are told to share and provide for three categories of people. With whom and in what proportion one gives varies with the needs God lays on the heart of each believer.

1. PROVIDING FOR DEPENDENTS

In our culture we are experiencing a tragic breakdown in this area of sharing. Husbands have failed to provide for their wives, parents have neglected their children, and grown sons and daughters have forsaken their elderly parents. Such neglect is solemnly condemned. "If anyone does not provide for his relatives, and especially for his immediate family, he has denied the faith and is worse than an unbeliever" (1 Timothy 5:8). Meeting the needs of your family is the first priority in sharing, and one on which there should be no compromise.

2. THE LOCAL CHURCH, CHRISTIAN WORKERS AND MINISTRIES

Throughout its pages, the Bible focuses on supporting the Lord's ministry. The Old Testament priesthood was to receive specific support (Numbers 18:21), and the New Testament teaching on ministry support is just as strong. "The elders who direct the affairs of the church well are worthy of double honour, especially those whose work is preaching and teaching" (1 Timothy 5:17). How many Christian workers have been distracted from their ministry by inadequate support? Far too many.

People ask if we should give only through our local church. In our case, the answer is no. However, we do give a minimum of 10 per cent of our regular income through our church because we believe this is a tangible expression of our commitment. But we also give to others who are directly having an influence on us. "Anyone who receives instruction in the word must share all good things with his instructor" (Galatians 6:6).

3. THE POOR

I didn't go to bed hungry last night, but conservative estimates are that 800 million people – that's more than 10 per cent of the world's population – go to bed hungry each night. In the UK it is reported that almost one million people use food banks. These numbers are so great – so many people feeling hopeless and wondering what they can do. That is overwhelming. Scripture consistently emphasises our responsibility to give to the poor and destitute.

In Matthew 14: 13-21 we read about how Jesus fed the 5,000. We are told that there were 5,000 men besides women and children, so maybe this should be looked at as the feeding of the 20,000 or some such other number. In any event, Jesus's miracle fed a lot of people. He used what was available to him – the young boy gave Jesus his five barley loaves and two small fish.

What can we learn? Well, Jesus made sure that everyone was fed. The wealthy, the poor, and the sick, those in front of Jesus where the food was multiplying and those at the very back. No one needed to go away as there was enough for all – and some left over. Jesus's message and provision is for all. The very cycle of nature and the earth that yields the harvest is His gift to all of us who inhabit the earth.

What can we do to help others who lack? What can you do personally? This is also our opportunity to give back to Jesus by helping those who are less fortunate. Jesus was tired yet still he found the time to help – often the needy know when to ask for help. The needy sometimes ask for more than you may have, but do not let that stop you giving help as Jesus never sent people away who needed His help. Sharing Jesus' love with someone can include meeting any kind of need, not just a spiritual one.

Have you brought your meagre broken pieces to Jesus?

When we bring our few resources to Him – and it passes through His hands – it becomes enough, more than enough, an abundance of blessings!

When we bring ourselves to Jesus Christ, it is absolutely miraculous what signs and wonders God can do through us!

What is holding you back from surrendering yourself and giving yourself and your gifts to God?

Matthew confronts us with one of the most exciting yet sobering truths in the Bible...

"Then the King will say...'For I was hungry and you gave me something to eat, I was thirsty and you gave me something to drink'.... Then the righteous will answer him, 'Lord, when did we see you hungry and feed you, or thirsty and give you something to drink?' The King will reply, 'I tell you the truth, whatever you did for one of the least of these brothers of mine, you did for me.' Then he will say to those on his left, 'Depart from me, you who are cursed, into the eternal fire...for I was hungry and you gave me nothing to eat, I was thirsty and you gave me nothing to drink...whatever you did not do for one of the least of these, you did not do for me.'" Matthew 25:34–45

THE GOOD SAMARITAN

The parable of the Good Samaritan in Luke 10:25-37 serves to remind us that we should reach out and help those who are in need. Ignoring those whom God calls us to minister to is not a Kingdom option. In Deuteronomy we read "Give generously to him and do so without a grudging heart; then because of this the Lord your God will bless you in all your work and in everything you put your hand to. There will always be poor people in the land. Therefore I command you to be open-handed towards your brothers and towards the poor and needy in your land" (Deuteronomy 15: 10-11). Isaiah the prophet declares God's commands to extend care to the poor, "If you extend your soul to the hungry and satisfy the afflicted soul, then your light shall dawn in the darkness, and your darkness shall be as the noonday. The Lord will guide you continually, and satisfy your soul in drought, and strengthen your bones;

you shall be like a watered garden, and like a spring of water, whose waters do not fail" (Isaiah 58:10-11).

Luke 12:33-34 says "Sell your possessions and give to the poor. Provide purses for yourselves that will not wear out, a treasure in heaven that will not be exhausted, where no thief comes near and no moth destroys. For where your treasure is, there your heart will be also." So even though the scale of global poverty might make you think that you can't have any impact, we need to give to the poor in obedience to God, and together we might just make a difference. In some mysterious way that we cannot fully comprehend, Jesus personally identifies with the poor. Do you want to minister to Christ? You do so when you give to the poor. If that truth is staggering, then the opposite is terrifying. When we do not give to the poor, we leave Christ Himself hungry and thirsty.

Three areas of our Christian life are affected by our giving or our lack of giving to the poor:

1. PRAYER

A lack of giving to the poor could be the cause of unanswered prayer. "Is not this the kind of fasting I have chosen. . . is it not to share your food with the hungry and to provide the poor wanderer with shelter...then you will call, and the Lord will answer" (Isaiah 58:6-9). And, "if a man shuts his ears to the cry of the poor, he too will cry out and not be answered" (Proverbs 21:13).

2. PROVISION

Our provision is conditional upon our giving to the needy. "He who gives to the poor will not lack, but he who hides his eyes will have many curses" (Proverbs 28:27, NKJ).

3. KNOWING JESUS CHRIST INTIMATELY

One who does not give to the poor does not know the Lord intimately. "He judged the cause of the poor and needy;

then it was well. Was not this knowing Me? says the Lord" (Jeremiah 22:16, NKJV).

With household finances stretched and consumerism having such a stranglehold, there often seems no place for giving to the poor. Nor should we assume that with the work of government agencies and the commitment of many excellent charities the poor are provided for. It was always God's intention that His people should be responsible for helping the poor, and around the country, churches are doing just that. A friend's church supports a maternity hospital in Shyira, Rwanda, and this initiative has received much support from the wider community. Other churches send practical support to Romania, support relief workers in Africa and much, much more. The passages just cited and the ministry of Jesus are evidence that giving must include giving to the poor. The first instinct of Zacchaeus when he met Jesus was to put his financial dealings in order and to serve the poor.

However, allow me to challenge you to pray that the Lord will bring one needy person into your life. This will be a significant step in the maturing of your relationship with the Lord. But giving to the poor goes beyond our direct personal experience. Could you give to a church programme that helps the poor? Should you give to a Christian agency that is supporting the poor through mission and relief work?

I pray that you and I might be able to echo Job's statement: "I rescued the poor who cried for help and the fatherless who had none to assist him...I made the widow's heart sing...I was eyes to the blind and feet to the lame. I was a father to the needy; I took up the case of the stranger" (Job 29:12-16).

We have one couple that we regularly give to – they are a couple who have little, the wife is handicapped and her husband does all he can to provide for his household. On other occasions we meet a need that we see or feel called to meet. Our church, like many churches, has programmes to assist those who are most in need. I have a very longstanding friend, Bob, who for over 20 years has laboured raising funds to help the poor and needy.

Although this area of giving can be frustrating at times, the potential benefits to the giver make it one of the most exciting and fulfilling areas in our entire Christian life.

PART 4 | CHAPTER 10

Tithing

For some, tithing is an old fashioned, religious sounding word that can be easily dismissed as an Old Testament command only; something that isn't particularly relevant to those of us who live under grace. But, and this is so important, it is a principle that existed and was practised before the law and continues under the new covenant.

Perhaps the most common reasons advanced for not accepting the need to tithe are as follows:

1.

Interesting. Such viewpoints are, I suggest advanced on many occasions by those who do not give 10 per cent or more. Tithing is a condition of the heart, not a money issue. It shows your surrender in the area of finance. Giving is not God's way of raising money. It's God's way of raising people into the likeness of His Son.

Proverbs tells us: "Honour the Lord with your wealth and with the first fruits of all your produce; then your barns will be filled with plenty, and your vats will be bursting with wine" (Proverbs 3: 9-10). Notice that Jesus doesn't say, 'You shouldn't have bothered about tithing when there are bigger matters to consider... '. He tells them that they were right to offer their tithe to God, but they were doing it for the wrong reasons. Tithing is a validation of your love for God, not a fear of Him.

In Mark 12: 41-44 Jesus comments on a poor widow who brought her offering into the temple treasury. "Jesus sat down opposite the place where the offerings were put and watched the crowd putting their money into the temple treasury. Many rich people threw in large amounts. But a poor widow came and put in two very small copper coins, worth only a few cents. Calling his disciples to him, Jesus said, "Truly I tell you, this poor widow has put more into the treasury than all the others. They all gave out of their wealth; but she, out of her poverty, put in everything—all she had to live on." Again Jesus focused on the heart of the giver. Here was a lady who understood the principle of being a giver. Nothing Jesus taught contradicts the giving of the tithe. Not one scripture confirms that Jesus or any other New Testament writer did not tithe or that we should not likewise do so.

Tithing is about more than just money; it's about putting God first, reaping His promise and living in His supply instead of trying to live under our own strength. By acting in faith, and bringing the first ten per cent of our increase back to God, we are saying "I know that I am in your hands God and don't want to live without you at the centre of what I do". By tithing we are acknowledging that God is our supplier and reminding ourselves of what He has done for us instead of focusing on what we might try and do for Him. If we can put our trust in God in the area of our finances and learn to be confident in His supply, how much easier will it be to trust in God's provision in all areas of our lives?

TITHING REDEEMS OUR LABOUR FROM FUTILITY

Just as we are freed from the curse of death and made right with God through Jesus, we can apply the same principle when it comes to our finances. When Adam disobeyed God, the earth, our supply, the work or toil of our hands was cursed. Our supply however can be released from this curse by tithing, by offering to God the first part of all our increase. The word tithe simply means a tenth and it is repeatedly stated in the Old Testament that God considers this first portion of our increase to be His, and as it belongs to God it is considered holy. When Jesus was sacrificed and given back to God, the rest of humanity was given the chance to put their faith in Him to be freed from the curse of death. So it is with tithing; by returning to God what is His, we release our financial supply from its curse and give God the opportunity to pour out His blessing upon the works of our hands. By giving God His portion, the remaining 90% becomes blessed.

A tithe of everything from the land, whether grain from the soil or fruit from the trees, belongs to the LORD; it is holy to the Lord (Leviticus 27:30).

If the part of the dough offered as first fruits is holy, then the whole batch is holy; if the root is holy, so are the branches (Romans 11:16).

BLESSED TO BE A BLESSING

When we tithe, God will cause the works of our hand to flourish so that we always have enough not just for ourselves, but so that we can always be generous to others. The tithe belongs to God, but we are also called to make free will offerings above and beyond the tithe; we are commanded to be generous to others.

EXPRESSING GOD'S CHARACTER

Our God is a generous God who sent His only Son as a sacrifice for us. Jesus gave up everything, His power and eventually His life for us. Why? So that we might become rich (2 Corinthians 8:9). We who believe in Him have inherited great riches: forgiveness, adoption, justification, the indwelling of the Holy Spirit, peace with God, access to God, sanctification and eternal glory to come. As Christ's disciples we should desire to be more like Him, and one way that we can do this is to give more.

GOD GAVE 100 PER CENT, SHOULD WE BE HAPPY WITH JUST 10 PER CENT?

God wants us to be generous like Him, not only because this type of life helps other people but because it makes our lives better too. God's Word tells us that generosity not only causes us to be more like Him but it makes our lives better as it brings refreshing and enlargement to our lives. Proverbs 11:24-25 puts it this way: "One man gives freely, yet gains even more; another withholds unduly, but comes to poverty. A generous man will prosper; he who refreshes others will himself be refreshed."

Being generous is living unselfishly, with concern for the wellbeing of others, free from a smallness of character or mind. This type of attitude is in direct opposition to our fallen human nature that is driven by self-interest and causes us to be miserly or jealous and hold onto our wealth. Therefore, with every generous act, we are suppressing our old nature and giving God's nature within us a chance to express itself. By living generously we convey God's character to the world that we live in.

PLAN TO BE GENEROUS

How long do you spend planning what you intend to give away? Does it even come close to the amount of time we spend planning what we can buy? Giving is something few learn to do naturally, but it is at the heart of God's purpose for us. Intense competition for our resources competes with the desire to give. Perhaps we do not give because opportunity denies us the opportunity to plan what to give away, or perhaps a deep-rooted belief that 'what is mine is mine' prevents us. What emotions do you experience when you are asked to give – unspeakable joy or feeling put on the spot?

WHAT DOES GOD THINK IF I DON'T TITHE?

Really the issue concerning tithing is not a financial issue rather it is one of obedience. If the Lord instructs us to tithe then, if we do not, we are disobeying God. How can the Lord bless us financially if we are not obedient to Him?

"Will a mere mortal rob God? Yet you rob me. "But you ask, 'How are we robbing you?' "In tithes and offerings. You are under a curse—your whole nation—because you are robbing me. Bring the whole tithe into the storehouse, that there may be food in my house. Test me in this," says the Lord Almighty, "and see if I will not throw open the floodgates of heaven and pour out so much blessing that there will not be room enough to store it." Malachi 3: 8-10

DOES GOD REALLY NEED YOUR MONEY?

No, what the Lord wants more than anything is for your heart to turn toward Him so that He can bless you. God's motive in His command for us to give is not for Him, it is for you and me.

Consider this

Growing in generosity

GET MORE INSIGHTS AT
→ WWW.YOURMONEYCOUNTS.ORG.UK

When we give we are obeying God.

Giving is an act of obedience that enables us to store up treasures in heaven.

Tithing has never been over written by any Scripture and remains central to God's requirement for His children.

When we give we show our gratitude to the Lord.

Giving strengthens our faith and enables us to live in freedom.

Key Questions

What truths have you learnt about giving that have been especially helpful?

How do you feel when you give?

Are you tithing into God's house?

Do you have a gift plan for the next 12 months? Maybe for your lifetime?

Do you give to the poor and needy?

Save.
Invest.
Spend.

Saving and investing | Spending | Standard of living | Perspectives

With so many transactions being made by card, and increasingly by swipe, keeping track of those card and bank balances is not always easy. If our finances are going to be ordered so that they are handled in a sound and godly manner, it is important to have a plan that you follow and adhere to as far as possible. Being intentional is essential if our finances are to be a source of blessing instead of something of a nightmare and worry.

Saving and investing

We are called to be wise stewards and a component of this includes saving money for future needs. Saving is the key that unlocks our ability to provide for the future. Saving sets funds aside for future spending. When you have savings you have options. There are always ways in which you can easily spend more than 100 per cent of your net disposable income, so saving requires denial and discipline.

WHAT'S THE DIFFERENCE BETWEEN SAVING AND INVESTING?

"Surely saving and investing are the same thing?" you might ask. Well, there is certainly some crossover in the minds of many. In order to establish the difference for the purposes of discovering what the Lord has to say about setting money aside: savings may be regarded as providing funds that you may wish or need to access in the short to medium-term, while investing is more long-term in its nature. You will be able to determine your definition of short- and long-term. Mine is up to five years for medium-term and I see more than five years as more long term. You might wish to regard all saving as investing – the key is the length of time and the purpose of the saving.

SOME PREVAILING CONCERNS AND ATTITUDES

- Some will say that we should not seek to store up or that saving could be viewed as hoarding.

- Others will say that it is more important to give rather than save.

- You might be disillusioned with low interest rates and think there is little point to saving, or that stock markets represent too much of a gamble, or feel a concern about the next market collapse and how long it might take for your money to grow back to previous levels.

- You might think of investing in buy to let property as a way to avoid low interest rates or the vagaries of stock markets. But stamp duty increases have significantly increased the initial cost of purchase, while being unable to deduct mortgage interest has greatly reduced the traditional return from buy to let investments.

- You might be struggling to make ends meet – "How can I possibly save?"

- You might be in debt, and again – "How can I possibly save?"

- You might have investments and feel that you do not have quite enough. You ask yourself the question: "How much is enough?" No matter how you look at this, it never seems as though you have enough.

- You might think it is important to live for today – after all there are so many ways to spend and so many people who wish you to buy their goods and services. The messages to spend are never-ending.

LET'S LOOK AT THE SAVING AND INVESTING BOTTOM LINES

Yes, I agree this is very simplistic but in essence having a saving and investment plan could look like this:

SAVING

This is to ensure that maybe you have enough set aside to cover your day-to-day costs if your main source of income were to cease. According to one source, the average person in our country is only two pay days away from bankruptcy. He or she has little or no money saved and has significant monthly credit obligations and a total dependence on next week's / month's income to keep the finances afloat.

How much? Maybe three months' net income. If possible maybe up to six months. Three months provides for any short term needs, while the six months may be seen as providing for a longer period without income.

These funds might also be vital in the event of having to unexpectedly replace a home appliance or pay for larger than expected car repair costs.

You might also save, as opposed to borrow, for something that you have purposed to buy - a new computer, change of car or a holiday?

INVESTING

How will you fund your living costs when work is no longer your calling at the beginning of the week? Most people find their retirement costs are somewhere in the region of 60-80% of pre-retirement expenditure - a financial cost that is probably greater than the state pension. And then there are the retirement dreams – that holiday perhaps. How will you spend your time? Will your hobbies cost or maybe earn you money?

It may be that you are focused on the here and now of today – work, family, health, church – and in terms of your priorities, setting aside today's money to plan for the future is not that high on your list. But it is important not to worry about the future or give no thought to the need to make ends meet in the latter years.

What teaching and principles on the handling of money and possessions are found in the Word of God that can help us answer our questions and point us toward saving and investing God's way?

SAVING - THE JOSEPH PRINCIPLE

The Bible tells us it's wise to save. "In the house of the wise are stores of choice food and oil, but a foolish man devours all he has" (Proverbs 21:20). Because of their instinct for saving, ants are commended for their wisdom: "Four things on earth are small, yet they are extremely wise: Ants are creatures of little strength, yet they store up their food in the summer" (Proverbs 30:24-25). They put aside and save from the summer's plenty to meet a future need. Saving is the opposite of being in debt. Saving is making provision for tomorrow, while debt is presumption upon tomorrow.

Another example is Joseph, who saved during the seven years of plenty to ensure there would be enough food during seven years of famine. I call saving the 'Joseph Principle'. Saving means to forego expenditure today so you will have something to spend in the future. Perhaps this is why some people never save; it requires a denial of something that you want today, and our culture is not a culture of denial. When we want something, we want it now.

SAVING FIRST STEPS

When you receive income, the first payment you should make is your tithe to the Lord and the second payment to your savings.

How often are our first two priorities the mortgage or rent and the housekeeping costs? Yes, they are important but maybe if we also prioritise the savings and tithe we will end up with something to give back to the Lord and something to save. This is why we need control of our money and possessions in a balanced spending plan.

> *The wise man saves for the future, but the foolish man spends whatever he gets.* Proverbs 21:20, TLB

The Bible does not tell us the amount or percentage to be saved. We recommend establishing a goal of saving at least 10 per cent of your income. For many at the beginning of adulthood this is not possible, but begin the habit of saving – even it is only a pound or two a month.

To develop this habit you can use several different methods. Some set aside a certain percentage of their regular income each month into a savings account, such as an Individual Savings Account (ISA). Some commit income from bonuses or overtime to their savings. Still others use an automatic savings plan or an employee payroll plan. Here is a maxim for saving: if you save a portion of your income as soon as you receive it, you will save more. There are four objectives for savings: (1) emergency fund, (2) short to medium-term, (3) long-term and (4) specific savings. Specific savings might for example be for the deposit on a house, a car replacement. For those with children it might be for wedding costs or to assist children with getting established in life.

BE A STEADY PLODDER

"Steady plodding brings prosperity; hasty speculation brings poverty" (Proverbs 21:5, TLB). The original Hebrew word for 'steady plodding' pictures a person filling a large barrel, one handful at a time. Little by little the barrel is filled to overflowing.

The fundamental principle you need to practise to become a successful investor is to spend less than you earn. Then save and invest the difference over a long period of time.

Examine those various investments that are well suited for 'steady plodding'. Your home mortgage is paid off after years of steady payments. A collective investment portfolio (e.g. unit trusts) is built as it is added to each month, and a business can increase steadily in value through the years as its growth, profitability and value are developed.

THE POWER OF COMPOUND GROWTH

I have always regarded this as the bedrock of an investment strategy. Save consistently, and maximise the advantage of compound growth. Compounding interest used to be referred to as the eighth wonder of the world when interest rates were higher. Regular saving combined with compound interest or income from dividends provides a return that varies based on the amount you save, the interest or dividend rate you earn on your savings, your tax position and the length of time you save.

1. THE AMOUNT

The amount you save will be determined by your disposable income, after the cost of your living, how much debt you have, your commitment to save and how faithfully you plan your finances, balancing your spending so that it is less than your income.

2. THE INTEREST OR GROWTH RATE

The second variable is the rate of interest or growth you earn on an investment. The following table demonstrates how an investment of £1,000 grows at various average rates of return.

As you can see, higher rates of return have a remarkable impact on the amount accumulated. A two per cent increase more than doubles the amount over 40 years. However, be wary of risky investments that promise a high return. It is an old maxim that informs us that the higher the return, the higher the risk. That risk might include fluctuating interest rates or dividend income fluctuations. Savings institutions have a tendency to change the terms of accounts and so this type of investment, simple as it is, will require a measure of monitoring.

Growth	Year 5	Year 10	Year 20	Year 30	Year 40
2%	1,105	1,221	1,491	1,821	2,224
4%	1,221	1,491	2,224	3,313	4,940
6%	1,348	1,821	3,313	6,023	10,957

The rates of return on deposit accounts are nowhere near as high as they were from the 1970s to 2008. The most important aspect is not the current rate of return but the fundamental importance of setting the funds aside.

3. TIME

Time is a factor we cannot control, but the graph that follows may help you visualise the benefits of starting now. If a person faithfully saves £2.74 each day – £1,000 per year – and earns 4 per cent on the savings, at the end of 40 years the savings will grow to almost £290,000 and will be earning almost £5,000 a year at a 3 per cent interest rate. Maybe by that time rates of interest or return will be higher. At a return of 8 per cent the investment would be worth over £290,000 and the annual income £23,200! Steady plodding pays. The message of the illustration is this: Start saving now!

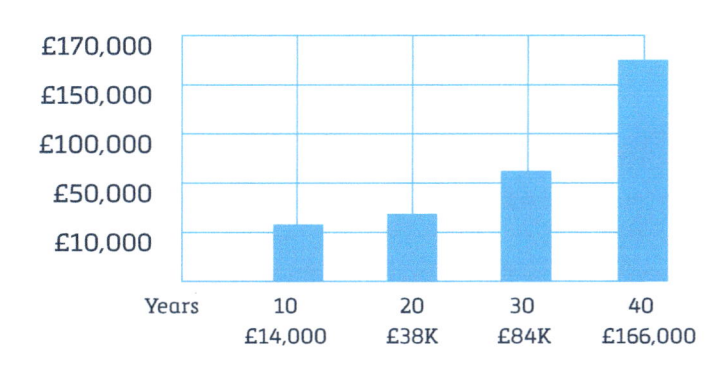

Years	10	20	30	40
	£14,000	£38K	£84K	£166,000

SCRIPTURE WARNS OF AVOIDING RISKY INVESTMENTS

"There is another serious problem I (Solomon) have seen everywhere – savings are put into risky investments that turn sour, and soon there is nothing left to pass on to one's son. The man who speculates is soon back to where he began – with nothing. This, as I said, is a very serious problem, for all his hard work has been for nothing; he has been working for the wind. It is all swept away." Ecclesiastes 5:13–16, TLB

Thousands of people lose money in highly speculative and sometimes fraudulent investments. How many times have you heard of older people losing their life savings on a get-rich-quick scheme? Sadly, it seems that Christians are particularly vulnerable to such schemes because they trust people who they think seem to live by the same values they have. I have known of investment scandals in churches where wolves in sheep's clothing fleeced the flock. There are three characteristics often associated with risky investments:

- The prospect of a large profit is 'practically guaranteed'

- The decision to invest must be made quickly. There will be no opportunity to thoroughly investigate the investment or the promoter who is selling the investment. The promoter will often be doing you a 'favour' by allowing you to invest

- Little will be said about the risks of losing money, and the investment will usually require no effort on your part.

Be patient when investing. There are few who have made money in a hurry and for all those who have, the road is littered with those who have lost money, and often a significant proportion of their savings. One person wrote to me saying, "I am a Christian living in the UK, I live in Surrey and work in London. I was sold an investment and was never told about the risk. Now it has gone wrong and I am facing bankruptcy." Diligence, study and counsel are prerequisites for improving your likelihood of making successful investments and avoiding risky ones.

DIVERSIFY

"Give portions to seven, yes to eight, for you do not know what disaster may come upon the land" (Ecclesiastes 11:2). There is no investment without risk, and Scripture does not recommend any specific investments. Money can be lost on any investment. A company can go into liquidation. Freehold property can suffer deflation. Money can be inflated until it is valueless.

The perfect investment does not exist. We need to diversify. Consider the following steps as you diversify. I recommend that you do not skip any of the steps. Start with step one, and take each step at a time.

Step 1: Save one month's living expenses.

Step 2: Save three to six months' living expenses; save for major purchases; develop your business and vocational skills. A principle in Scripture is to invest in your business or vocation, which will be productive, then build your house: "Develop your business first before building your house" (Proverbs 24:27, TLB). Many people today reverse this order. The large house, purchased too early in life, tends to require so much money that investing in business or vocation is seriously hampered.

Step 3: Purchase a home; invest conservatively to meet long term goals.

Step 4: Make other investments.

When it comes to investing, there is more to life than ISAs, stocks and shares.

COUNT THE COST

With every investment there are costs: financial costs, time commitments and efforts required. Sometimes investments can bring emotional stress. Before you decide on any investment, carefully consider all the costs.

Saving and giving go hand in hand.

It is scripturally permissible to save and invest only when we are also giving. Jesus told a parable that illustrates the danger of saving while not giving.

"The ground of a certain rich man produced a good crop. He thought to himself, 'What shall I do? I have no place to store my crops.' Then he said, 'This is what I'll do. I will tear down my barns and build bigger ones, and there I will store all my grain and my goods. And I'll say to myself, 'You have plenty of good things laid up for many years. Take life easy; eat, drink and be merry." But God said to him, 'You fool! This very night your life will be demanded from you. Then who will get what you have prepared for yourself?' This is how it will be with anyone who stores up things for himself but is not rich towards God.... For where your treasure is; there your heart will be also." (Luke 12:16–21, 34)

The key word in this parable is 'all'. Jesus called the rich man a fool because he saved all of his goods, laying them up for his own use. He did not balance his saving by giving generously. It is legitimate to save and invest only when we are also giving to the Lord. Why? "Where your treasure is, there your heart will be also" (Matthew 6:21).

If we concentrate solely on saving and investing, our focus and affection will gravitate there. We will be drawn inexorably to those possessions. But if we balance our saving and investing by giving generously to the Lord, we can still love Christ first with all our heart.

PLANNING YOUR GIVING

1. PROVIDING FOR YOUR FAMILY

Paul writes in 1 Timothy 5:8 "if anyone does not provide for his relatives, and especially for his immediate family, he has denied the faith and is worse than an unbeliever." This principle extends to providing for your needs in old age and leaving an inheritance to your children.

2. BECOMING FINANCIALLY FREE TO SERVE THE LORD

One objective of saving is to diminish our dependence upon a salary to meet our needs. This affords the freedom to volunteer more time to ministry should this be what the Lord wants for us. The more my savings produce, the less I am dependent upon income from my work. Some have saved enough to be free one day a week and others are in a position to be full-time volunteers without the need to earn a salary.

3. SEEKING TO BLESS OTHERS

The Bible tells us that it is more blessed to give than receive. I can certainly agree with that but there are those who are happy to receive. An extreme example are those who fund themselves by begging on the street. Those who sell the Big Issue are grateful not only for the sale but also anything extra that might come their way. I have heard others share how grateful and blessed they were to receive a gift – often these are anonymous gifts. Look at the instruction we have from Matthew 6: 3-4 "But when you give to the needy, do not let your left hand know what your right hand is doing, so that your giving may be in secret. Then your Father, who sees what is done in secret, will reward you."

UNACCEPTABLE INVESTMENT GOALS

According to Paul in 1 Timothy 6:9–11 one investment goal, the desire to become rich, is strictly prohibited. "People who want to get rich fall into temptation and a trap and into many foolish and harmful desires that plunge men into ruin and destruction." Study this carefully and beware! The prohibition against wanting to get rich in 1 Timothy 6:9 is followed by this passage: "For the love of money is a root of all kinds of evil" (1 Timothy 6:10). In other words, when we want to get rich, Scripture tells us that we are loving money.

I never planned to become rich. My businesses enabled me to enjoy a measure of financial success, but most of the financial rewards were not spent, they were saved. What did that achieve? At the time they did offer a measure of security within the business, but now I realise that God's plan was for me to serve Him in full-time ministry and to use the assets He entrusted to us for His purposes. Do I think I have always been a faithful steward? If I had known earlier in life what I know now, then I would certainly have done better. However, I have discussed this subject with Rhoda and we conclude that even though I didn't have the understanding I do now, I have run the financial race so far fairly well. However, if asked the question, could I have given more away, then the answer is certainly 'yes'! I am not so sure that giving is as natural as it first appears. However, it is unquestionably at the heart of God's economy.

This chapter is about investing, so let us return to our subject matter! When I focus on being a faithful steward, I am Christ-centred in my thoughts and attitudes. My actions are then motivated by a pure heart. I am serving Christ and growing closer to Him.

Matthew 6:24 says, "no-one can serve two masters. Either he will hate the one and love the other, or he will be devoted to the one and despise the other. You cannot serve both God and money." When we want to get rich, we are actually loving money and hating God. We are holding on to money and despising God. We are serving money, and we are therefore not serving the living God. 1 Timothy 6:10 ends by saying, "some people, eager for money, have wandered from the faith and pierced themselves with many griefs."

Toward the end of a recent stay in Atlanta, I read in a national newspaper, **USA Today**, one of its snapshot surveys. The survey question of the day addressed to those earning $50,000 asked "how much do you need to earn to be comfortable?" The average answer was $75,000 – an increase of 50%. The same question was asked of those earning $100,000 and their response was $250,000, an increase of 250%. What conclusion might be drawn from this survey? Enough is never enough – the love of money is never satisfied.

One of my core beliefs when I was building the businesses was that I was not in business to make money. I determined that my priorities in business were, firstly, to meet and exceed the needs of my customers and, secondly, to provide a happy and challenging workplace for my employees.

I decided that the extent to which I achieved these goals would be directly reflected in profits. I believe that the purpose of a business is to meet the needs of its customers, and one of the outcomes of achieving that is that the business will be successful, and one of the results of being successful is that the business will make a profit. Thus one of my benchmarks was profit and not money. The difference? For me, it was all down to attitude and focus: if all you ever do is to focus on the bottom line, you run the risk of missing out on opportunities to grow the business and increase profitability.

There is nothing wrong with having wealth as this is a consequence of being a faithful steward. However, the Bible is replete with warnings against the love of money. In God's economy there is an emphasis on giving.

SPLIT AND SUBMIT

We overcome the temptation to get rich by remembering to split and submit. In 1 Timothy 6:11 Paul counsels Timothy to, "flee from all this [the desire to get rich], and pursue righteousness, godliness, faith, love, endurance and gentleness." When you become aware of your desire to become rich, you must split (remove yourself) from that temptation and replace it with the pursuit of godliness.

Next, submit. The ultimate way to escape is found in submitting to Jesus as Lord. We can do this in perfect confidence because Jesus did not succumb to any temptation to become rich. After Christ fasted 40 days in the wilderness, the devil tempted Him three times. The final temptation is recorded in Luke 4:5-7: "the devil led him up to a high place and showed him in an instant all the kingdoms of the world. The devil said to him "I will give you all their authority and splendour,...if you worship me, it will all be yours."

Can you imagine what an incredible temptation this would present?

GAMBLING AND LOTTERIES

The Gambling Commission reports that over 70 per cent of adults gamble. The National Lottery accounts for 55 per cent while other forms of gambling have over 50 per cent of adults admitting to engaging in them. Gambling on the internet is growing exponentially and more and more young adults are being drawn into gaming – which surely must be seen as 'grooming' for gambling.

How much is spent in the UK on gambling? A recent survey indicates that almost £7 billion is spent gambling on the National Lottery. That amounts to more than £150 per household.

Sadly, there are hundreds of thousands of compulsive gamblers who regularly deplete their family income. Their stories are heart-breaking. The Bible does not specifically prohibit gambling; however, many who gamble do so in an attempt to get rich quickly. This is a violation of Scripture.

As men and women who serve a holy God, we are called to be salt and light to a lost world. I firmly believe we need to make a commitment never to participate in gambling or lotteries even for entertainment. We should not expose ourselves to the risk of becoming compulsive gamblers, nor should we support an industry that enslaves so many.

INHERITANCE

Parents should attempt to leave a material inheritance for their children's children: "a good man leaves an inheritance for his grandchildren" (Proverbs 13:22). The inheritance should not be dispensed until the child has been thoroughly trained to be a wise steward: "an inheritance quickly gained at the beginning will not be blessed at the end" (Proverbs 20:21).

You should also provide for the inheritance to be distributed over several years or when the heir is mature enough to handle the responsibility of money. Some Wills do not provide for a fully accessible inheritance until the age of 18, 21 or sometimes beyond. In these circumstances a Will often provides for the establishment of a trust with trustees appointed to help supervise the use of those funds.

You should provide an inheritance for your children. However, it probably is not wise to leave your children with great wealth if they have not been thoroughly schooled in the biblical perspective of money and how to manage it properly. I have known wealthy individuals who were concerned about the effect their wealth would have in the hands of their children. I am sure you can think of heirs and heiresses whose behaviour might cause concern if they were your children. An inheritance can turn out to be a curse. No one has the right to handicap their children with such a burden as great wealth. They must face this question squarely: will the fortune be safe with my child, and will my child be safe with my fortune?

Many people who die do not have an up-to-date Will. It is often reported that about 20 per cent of adults do not have a Will. Think of what this means. To die without a Will is expensive and time consuming and can be heart-breaking for your loved ones. It can literally destroy an estate left to provide for the family.

Scripture teaches that we brought nothing into the world and we will take nothing with us when we die, but we can leave behind our money and possessions precisely as we wish. We can specify to whom and how much. If you die without a Will, these decisions become subject to intestacy law which may, and almost certainly will, result in your estate being distributed in a way that would not meet with your wishes. If you leave minor children, it will be Social Services who decide who will look after them. In that case, they may select someone who may not know the Lord. In order to encourage clients to make a Will, I used to ask them if they would like the government to decide who should look after their children. I cannot recall a client who who did not then make out their Will.

Whether you are married or single, rich or poor, you should have a Will. Not only does it clear up any legal 'uncertainties', it also helps you map out your finances while you are alive so that you can protect the best interests of your heirs.

About one in six of the population dies before retirement age. So do not put off preparation of your Will just because you may be young. Do it now! As Isaiah told Hezekiah: "this is what the Lord says: put your house in order, because you are going to die; you will not recover" (2 Kings 20:1). One of the greatest gifts you can leave your family for that emotional time will be an organised estate and a properly prepared Will. If you do not have a current Will, please make an appointment with a solicitor to prepare one.

Spending

DO YOU HAVE A SPENDING PLAN?

Yes, you're right – that is another way of enquiring if you have a budget! However, we will use the term 'spending plan' just in case you are averse to the term 'budget'. It is an often used word – but it is not a word that trips lightly off of everyone's lips without bringing with it a sense of failure or hopelessness.

When you start off on a journey you may once have needed to refer to a map to write out your plan. Then the internet gave us route maps which seemed to have one instruction for every mile. Now most people who are accustomed to going on longer journeys have access to a sat nav. The purpose of the sat nav is to help you arrive at the intended destination in the shortest time – at least that is, I think, the intention. There is an old saying that reminds us that if you do not know where you are going any route will get you there.

If you decide to go abroad you will probably create a travel itinerary so that you know what time you are leaving and how to connect with your preferred transport to your destination.

How many people go to the supermarket without a shopping list?

Plans. Plans. Plans. In order to get it right the sat nav, the itinerary and the shopping list are your plans. Your spending plan is no different but do you have one, and do you keep to it? Is it a well-balanced plan? Does it have any margin for the unexpected?

You might not be very good with money. Well, you are not alone – I am a chartered accountant who does not find handling cash easy at all. My youngest son is also a chartered accountant and when I was out with him recently he confided that he used cards for everything as he was hopeless with cash. [Note to myself – could have done a better job in training him how to handle cash. Incidentally, that is, of course, the problem with cards. Want something. Need something. Out comes the card with very little thought as to the spending plan.]

I have helped many people over the years with sorting out their finances. Experience has taught me not to take over others' journey to financial freedom. Much better to allow biblical principles and the believer's own sense of doing what is right and godly to prevail than to say, "do this or do that". Never again will I take away the responsibility of developing the spending plan – to my mind if you create it, you will own it and you will be committed to keeping to it, and you can rejoice

> *Annual income twenty pounds, annual expenditure nineteen pounds nineteen and six, result happiness. Annual income twenty pounds, annual expenditure twenty pounds nought and six, result misery.*
> *Charles Dickens*

in keeping to it. What if you fall short? Pick yourself up and recommit – failure is not an option. Besides, God sees you as a success, so align your thoughts with God's view of you.

YOUR SITUATION

You might be a student, employed or self-employed. You might be a business manager, a business owner, retired - maybe newly or facing imminent retirement. You may be living on welfare benefits. Whatever your situation, handling money and making spending decisions are an everyday fact of life.

All you can do is create a plan whilst knowing that all plans will come under strain. The key is to create a plan that has as much margin as possible.

We will look at this as you work through creating your own plan. But for now, it is important to somehow develop your own view regarding your objectives/goals/dreams. These probably include planning to make expenditure less than income, downsizing debt, giving and saving. This is not a self-help guide rather a guide to what the Lord has written. The setting is an understanding of twenty-first century economics and reality, the foundation is the Bible.

WHY PREPARE A SPENDING PLAN?

Creating a spending plan is probably not many people's first choice way of spending time, but it is the only way to follow through and apply what has been learned about getting out of debt, saving and giving while still meeting basic personal and household needs. Balancing income and expenditure and either staying out of debt or getting out of debt comprise some of the essentials of good housekeeping. Your spending plan will allow you to plan the priorities of the household costs, giving and saving and other needs and expenditures. Regardless of income, many have difficulty making ends meet unless there is a plan for spending. Costs always seem to rise just a little more than income. I have seen many examples of this. Regardless of what a person earns, they may well struggle toward the end of the week or month unless there is a spending plan in place that is accompanied by a disciplined approach to spending. Creating a spending plan introduces a financial discipline in your spending that is needed to reach financial objectives. If you are in a mess financially it is probably the misfortune of circumstance maybe combined with a measure of indiscipline that has resulted in your current situation. You are not the only one – it is common for financial problems to arise over a period of time. In that sense it is a little like being overweight – that happens over time – and as with dieting getting your figure back in shape takes time so does getting your finances back in order. So, in that sense maybe you are thinking of going on a financial diet. Hhhm, not so sure that is a good analogy, but you get my point! Back to the Bible...

Working on your spending plan provides an opportunity to pray about spending decisions. This is important because, according to one survey, more than 70 per cent of marital breakdowns cite financial mismanagement as one of the prime or contributory causes. I seldom see a family with financial problems where there is not real tension within the home.

A successful plan should be a joint effort. It is a good communication tool for the husband and wife to use. A plan also can help a family achieve full value for its money without losing sight of the things family members want most.

I know one church family that is committed to sending their children to youth camp each summer for a week. Several years ago, as they were making their annual spending plans in January, it became apparent that there would not be enough money for the children to go to youth camp. The family then agreed everyone would 'contribute' to camp by making a sacrifice: the father gave up his monthly game of golf, the mother did not join her tennis club, and the children received half their normal pocket money. By using their plan, the family was able to anticipate a problem and adjust their spending to enable them to get what they wanted most – in this case going off to youth camp.

HOW TO PLAN

A spending plan is useful only if it is used. It should be a plan specifically tailored for managing your finances, not someone else's. Some people are more comfortable using a handwritten system, while others prefer using a budget system on a spreadsheet.

To prepare your plan, follow these three steps:

STEP ONE – START WHERE YOU ARE NOW

Developing a spending plan must begin with your current situation. Determine exactly how much household income and expenditure you have. Some people do not know what they are actually earning and spending. For this reason it is essential to keep a record of every penny spent for a week/month to gain an accurate picture in order to complete a first version of your plan.

If your wages or salary are not the same each month (perhaps you have income which is partly commission based, or you work overtime, or maybe you have a zero hour contract), make a conservative estimate of your annual income and divide by 12 to establish a working figure for your monthly income.

Then determine which expenses do not necessarily occur each month. Examples are water and gas/electricity, holidays, birthdays and Christmas. Estimate how much these cost for a year and divide that amount by 12 to determine your monthly cost. If you have not kept your bills or receipts, check with your bank and/or credit statement records to see how much you paid. Armed with this information, you can complete the Estimated Weekly/Monthly Spending Plan on one of the following two pages. Do not be discouraged. Almost every spending plan starts out with expenditure in excess of income. But a solution exists.

STEP TWO – THE SOLUTION IS WHERE WE WANT TO BE

To solve the problem of spending more than your income, you must either increase your income or decrease your expenditure. It is that simple: you need to either earn more or spend less.

INCREASING YOUR INCOME

A part-time job, or possibly a project that would involve others in the family, are ways of increasing your income. The ever-present danger of increasing income is the tendency for expenses also to rise. To avoid this problem, agree to apply any additional income to balancing spending so that it becomes less than income. Another potential concern is the effect that dedicating more time to work will have on relationships, both within the family and outside, in order to earn more money. The 'pain' in order to make the 'gain' needs to be considered. If you have a zero hour contract – keep looking for that job with greater income security.

REDUCING YOUR EXPENDITURE

When I was running my accountancy firm I had many clients who were in seasonal businesses. Some owned holiday lets, others were in the fishing tackle and garden centre trades. Whenever I was involved with cash flow planning for seasonal businesses we would always look at the ability of the business to pay an even amount of income to the owner throughout the year. There was no point in taking high income during the busy times only to find there was no spare cash when the prime season had past. I also had actor clients and many of them would have other employment in between their acting engagements.

If you do have fluctuating income as mentioned already, prepare your plan taking a pessimistic viewpoint of your income. Which items of expenditure are absolutely necessary? Which can you do without? Which can you reduce?

PART 5 | CHAPTER 12

ESTIMATED WEEKLY BUDGET
Budget - keep abreast of the facts

Gross Income
Gross income: _____
Salary _____
Benefits _____
Dividends _____
Other income _____

Deduct:
1. Giving: _____
2. Taxes: _____
3. Other deduction: _____ _____

Net Spendable Income A: _____

Living Expenses
4. Housing: _____
Mortgage/rent _____
Insurance _____
Council tax _____
Electricity _____
Gas _____
Water/sewerage _____
Telephone _____
Maintenance _____
Garden supplies _____
Other _____

5. Food/supermarket: _____

6. Transport: _____
Payments _____
Fuel _____
Insurance _____
Vehicle duty _____
Repair replacement _____
Other _____

7. Insurance: _____
Life _____
Sickness _____
Other _____

8. Debts: _____
(except car and mortgage)

9. Entertainment/recreation: _____
Babysitters _____
Holidays _____
Pets _____
Other _____

10. Clothing: _____

11. Savings: _____

12. Medical costs: _____
Dentist _____
Prescriptions _____
Other _____

13. Miscellaneous*: _____
Toiletries/cosmetics* _____
Laundry/cleaning _____
Allowances _____
Subscriptions _____
Birthdays/anniv. _____
Events _____
Christmas presents _____
Postage _____
Professional/legal _____
Other _____

14. School/childcare: _____
Tuition _____
Day care _____
Other _____

15. Investments: _____

Total Living Expenses £ _____

Income vs. Living costs

Net Spendable Income: **A** _____

Deduct: Total living expenses: **B** _____

Surplus or Deficit: £ _____

*Where not included in the supermarket account

157

BOUGHT

ESTIMATED MONTHLY BUDGET
Budget - keep abreast of the facts

Gross Income
Gross income: _____
Salary _____
Benefits _____
Dividends _____
Other income _____

Deduct:
1. Giving: _____
2. Taxes: _____
3. Other deduction: _____ _____

Net Spendable Income A: _____

Living Expenses
4. Housing: _____
Mortgage/rent _____
Insurance _____
Council tax _____
Electricity _____
Gas _____
Water/sewerage _____
Telephone _____
Maintenance _____
Garden supplies _____
Other _____

5. Food/supermarket: _____

6. Transport: _____
Payments _____
Fuel _____
Insurance _____
Vehicle duty _____
Repair replacement _____
Other _____

7. Insurance: _____
Life _____
Sickness _____
Other _____

8. Debts: _____
(except car and mortgage)

9. Entertainment/recreation: _____
Babysitters _____
Holidays _____
Pets _____
Other _____

10. Clothing: _____

11. Savings: _____

12. Medical costs: _____
Dentist _____
Prescriptions _____
Other _____

13. Miscellaneous*: _____
Toiletries/cosmetics* _____
Laundry/cleaning _____
Allowances _____
Subscriptions _____
Birthdays/anniv. _____
Events _____
Christmas presents _____
Postage _____
Professional/legal _____
Other _____

14. School/childcare: _____
Tuition _____
Day care _____
Other _____

15. Investments: _____

Total Living Expenses £ _____

Income vs. Living costs

Net Spendable Income: **A** _____

Deduct: Total living expenses: B _____

Surplus or Deficit: £ _____

*Where not included in the supermarket account

Here are some suggestions to help you evaluate your major expenses. In order to take a preliminary view of your spending, please check out yourmoneycounts.org for some cost-saving ideas. Here are a few suggestions about costs that are included in most household plans.

ACCOMMODATION

1. Purchase an older house you can improve by yourself. Perhaps consider a smaller house suitable to your needs today with a design that can be expanded to meet your future needs.

2. Consider apartment living. It can be less expensive and involves fewer responsibilities – garden care, maintenance, etc.

3. If you can do your own repair and maintenance work such as garden care, car cleaning, painting and carpet cleaning, you will save a substantial amount.

4. Shop carefully for furniture and household appliances. Car boot sales are a good source of reasonably priced household goods.

5. Which appliances could be switched off? Double glazing and roof insulation reduce energy consumption. Good housekeeping can save 15% of your energy supplies, so make sure you don't leave appliances on. Even if you leave the plug in the socket, this uses up energy!

6. Lower the cost of your energy supplies by limiting the use of heating, lights and appliances. See energysavingtrust.org.uk for more details.

BOUGHT

FOOD

1. Be careful with supermarket offers – especially where perishable food is concerned.

2. Prepare a menu for the week. Then list the ingredients from the menu and shop according to the list. This will help you plan a nutritionally balanced diet, avoid impulse shopping and eliminate waste.

3. Shop once a week. Each time we go shopping for 'some little thing', we always seem to buy 'some other little thing' as well. Would a different discount supermarket reduce the cost of the shopping?

4. Reduce the number of ready meals, which have expensive packaging added to the cost.

5. Leave children and hungry spouses at home when shopping. The fewer distractions the better.

6. Lunches eaten out are often spending plan breakers. A lunch prepared at home and taken to work will help reduce costs and the waistline.

7. Reduce the use of disposable products. Paper plates, cups and napkins are expensive to use.

TRANSPORT

1. If it is possible to get by with one car, this will be the biggest cost reduction.

2. Purchase a low-cost and low-mileage used car and drive it until repairs become too expensive.

3. The smaller the car, the more economical to operate. You pay an estimated 25 to 40 per cent of the current value of your car each year in total vehicle related costs.

Assuming average annual mileage, the cost to run a car per mile averages over 45p a mile.

4. Perform routine maintenance yourself – oil changes, lubrication, etc. Regular maintenance will prolong the life of your car.

CLOTHING

1. Make a written list of your yearly clothing needs. Shop from the list during the sales, or at lower cost clothing shops.

2. Purchase simple basic fashion items that stay in style longer rather than clothes that will soon be out of season.

3. Do not purchase a lot of clothing. Select one or two basic colours for your wardrobe, and buy outfits that you can wear in combination with others.

4. Purchase home-washable fabrics. Clothes that must be commercially cleaned are expensive to maintain.

INSURANCE

1. Select insurance based on your need and affordability, check the costs at a number of online sites, making comparisons from at least three major insurance companies.

2. Raising the insurance excess feature will substantially reduce premiums but that needs to be balanced against the likelihood of a claim arising. You will need to have savings to ensure that paying the excess does not upset your spending plan.

3. Seek the recommendation of friends for a good insurance agent. A capable agent can save you money. However, make sure you check their rates with those comparable online.

HEALTH

1. Practice preventive medicine. Your body will stay healthier when you get the proper amount of sleep and exercise, and have a balanced diet. Less sugar, less fat, less alcohol will enable you to better maintain your health as well as save money

2. Practice proper oral hygiene for healthy teeth and to reduce dental bills.

ENTERTAINMENT AND RECREATION

1. Plan your holidays if you can for the off-peak season and select destinations near home.

2. Rather than expensive entertainment, seek creative alternatives such as picnics or visits to the local parks.

FIVE TIPS

1. Reconcile your bank statement with your bank payments and receipts each month.

2. It is helpful to have a separate savings account where you can deposit the monthly standing order for the bills that do not arise each month. For example, if your annual insurance premium is £480, deposit £40 in this savings account each month. This ensures the money will be available when these payments become due. But be careful to ensure that your direct debit cost is not loaded with charges from the insurance company.

3. We are trained to think how we are paid – either weekly or monthly. To better understand the impact of an expense, calculate the yearly cost. For example, if you spend £4 for lunch each working day, multiply by five days a week by 46 weeks a year. That gives an annual

cost of over £900. Even a coffee a day could cost more than £450 a year. Thinking annually provides a different perspective on those small 'inconsequential' costs.

4. Control your impulse-spending. Impulse-spending ranges from buying expensive items like cars to smaller items such as the latest smartphone. Each time you have the urge to spend for something not planned, post it to an 'impulse list' and pray about the purchase for several days. As you do this, the impulse will often pass.

5. It is wise for husbands and wives to include personal allowances in the plan. Both should be given allowances to spend as they please. Spend within the plan – not a penny more!

STEP THREE – DO NOT STOP!

The most common temptation is to stop the planning and the adherence to it. Don't. Many people find it difficult to create a balanced spending plan by themselves. If you have not yet enrolled in a **Your Money Counts** small group study, I strongly encourage you to do so. If there is no small group studying the five part '**Money or Maker**' study, maybe you could start one. Visit yourmoneycounts.org for further information. In the small group environment you will be encouraged, yet held accountable to implement biblical financial principles and good budgeting habits.

Remember, a spending plan is simply a plan for spending your money. It will not work by itself. Every area of your plan should be regularly reviewed to keep a rein on spending. "Any enterprise is built by wise planning, becomes strong through common sense, and profits wonderfully by keeping abreast of the facts" (Proverbs 24:3-4, TLB). There may well be frustrations, but a spending plan, if properly used, will save you hundreds, maybe thousands of pounds. It will help you accumulate savings (because spending includes saving) and will help you stay out of debt. More importantly, it will help husbands and wives communicate in an area that is a leading cause of marital stress or even conflict.

# Standard of living

HOW SHALL WE THEN LIVE?

How do you feel about the possibility of balancing the spending with your income? Remember – it is possible. Your detailed record of what you have spent in a month is one important key to think about how you spend your income. If we follow God's blueprint for giving, it may well be that you have to reduce your expenditure - this is especially the case if you also are going to commit to downsize the burden of debt.

Remember, you are not alone in facing this challenge. If you are a student – can you confide in your parent(s)? If you have lost your life partner – who could you ask for help? Adult children or perhaps a trusted church friend? Have you looked at the yourmoneycounts.org website for help? Above all – study His Word and pray. How to pray? Ask for forgiveness if you feel you have made a real mess, and then receive that forgiveness and do not look back, for He is faithful and will forgive. Remove the enemy's taunt of failure. Develop your plan. Resist the temptations of the world, and be content.

It is not unnatural to want to "live a better life". That, after all, is the message of the Bible, except the Bible's message is not about spending and having this or that, it is about receiving that which is freely given. As you further advance your understanding of the Word and its applicability to your own situation, let's explore what else we can glean from the Bible about what we call today, our 'standard of living'.

THINK WITH AN ETERNAL PERSPECTIVE

Nurture an eternal perspective. Our culture and the media implore us to focus on the here and now. Advertisers persuade consumers to gratify themselves today with no thought of tomorrow. Examine the following to understand how brief life is on earth compared with eternity.

Our momentary time on earth is but a dot on the timeline of eternity. Yet we have the opportunity to influence eternity by how we handle money today. We have not only the privilege to lay up treasures for ourselves in heaven but also the opportunity to spend money to influence people for Jesus Christ. Gaining an eternal perspective and eternal values will have a profound effect on your decision making.

Moses is a good example. Let's look at Hebrews 11:24–26: "By faith Moses, when he had grown up, refused to be known as the son of Pharaoh's daughter. He chose to be ill-treated along with the people of God rather than to enjoy the pleasures of sin for a short time. He regarded disgrace for the sake of Christ as of greater value than the treasures of Egypt, because he was looking ahead to his reward."

Moses faced a choice. As Pharaoh's adopted son he could enjoy the lavish lifestyle of royalty, or he could choose to become a Hebrew slave. Because he had an eternal perspective, he chose the latter and was used by the Lord in a remarkable way. We face a similar decision. We can either live with a view toward eternity or live focused on this present world.

Have you ever returned to a place you knew as a child? I once visited a recreation ground where I played when I was 12 years old. I remembered it as a huge field surrounded by fences and a railway line. I was amazed to discover how small it really was! Or do you remember wanting to get something so much you could almost taste it? Yet today it means almost nothing to you. I think we will experience something similar after we arrive in heaven. Many things that seem so important to us now will fade into insignificance in the light of eternity.

YOU ARE A PILGRIM

Scripture tells us about our identity and role on earth: first of all, we are citizens of heaven, not earth (Philippians 3:20). Second, we are ambassadors representing Christ on this earth (2 Corinthians 5:20). Third, we are aliens, strangers and pilgrims on this earth (Hebrews 11:13).

Peter wrote, "since you call on a Father who judges each man's work impartially, live your lives as strangers here in reverent fear" (1 Peter 1:17).

Later he added, "I urge you, as aliens and strangers in the world, to abstain from sinful desires, which war against your soul" (1 Peter 2:11). The pilgrim is a traveller and not a settler – one who is acutely aware that the excessive accumulation of things can only distract from reaching the goal or destination. Material possessions are valuable to a pilgrim only if they facilitate the mission. The pilgrim is a traveller who chooses possessions strategically, regarding most of them as encumbrances that would slow the journey or make it impossible. Of course, many of us become "settlers" in the temporal sense, living in houses, owning furniture and developing businesses. There is nothing wrong with this, but we need to maintain a pilgrim mentality of detachment – the traveller's philosophy of travelling light. Acquire only those possessions that enable you to fulfil God's calling on your life.

MAKE AN EFFORT TO LIVE SIMPLY

Every possession requires time, attention and often money to maintain it. Too many or the wrong types of possessions can demand so much time, energy or money that they consume our time and maybe harm our relationship with the Lord and others. The quiet, simple life is the best environment to allow us enough time to nurture our relationship with the Lord.

Paul, in 1 Thessalonians 4:11-12, counsels: "Make it your ambition to lead a quiet life, to mind your own business and to work with your hands, just as we told you, so that your daily life may win the respect of outsiders and so that you will not be dependent on anybody."

WE ARE AT WAR

"Endure hardship with us like a good soldier of Christ Jesus. No one serving as a soldier gets involved in civilian affairs – he wants to please his commanding officer" (2 Timothy 2:3-4). In the Second World War, people changed their lifestyles radically to help win the war. They rationed the use of strategically important items. They spent less on life's comforts so that the army would be adequately supplied. As soldiers, we should be careful not to become unduly encumbered with the cares of this life.

RECOGNISE THE ENEMY

"For our struggle is not against flesh and blood, but...against the powers of this dark world and against the spiritual forces of evil in the heavenly realms" (Ephesians 6:12). In a war you are going to use your most effective weapon. The devil's mission is to divert us from serving Christ. He frequently accomplishes this by tempting us to serve money and possessions. As we have seen before, money is the primary competitor with Christ for the lordship of our life. "You cannot serve both God and money" (Matthew 6:24).

Serving money is often difficult to recognise because loving money is a 'respectable' sin – people will congratulate you for acquiring the trappings of financial success. Therefore, you should prayerfully examine your relationship with Christ and money.

SPEND IN A WAY THAT PLEASES THE LORD

Prayerfully submit spending decisions to the Lord. Everything we possess is owned by Him, and we should spend to please Him and not for a selfish purpose. Seeking the

Lord's direction in spending does not mean that we will never spend for anything other than a basic necessity. Recreation, appropriate leisure activities and rest are important. "Since everything God created is good, we should not reject any of it but receive it with thanks" (1 Timothy 4:4, NLT).

DO NOT WASTE POSSESSIONS

"There was a rich man whose manager was accused of wasting his possessions. So he called him in and asked him 'what is this I hear about you? Give an account of your management, because you cannot be manager any longer'" (Luke 16:1-2). Examine yourself. Do you spend money frivolously or waste possessions habitually?

DO NOT COMPARE YOURSELF TO OTHERS

Some use comparison with others to justify spending more than they should. Many have suffered financially because they tried but could not afford to 'keep up with the Joneses'. Someone once said, "You can never keep up with the Joneses. Just about the time you catch them, they remortgage their home and go deeper in debt to buy more things!" If you are wealthy, your lifestyle should be based on the conviction that the Lord wants you to have a certain standard of living that is not necessarily dictated by the maximum you can afford.

IF ONLY I HAD MORE...

Have you ever felt that if only you were in a more prestigious position or had more money, then you could accomplish really significant things for the Lord?

Let's examine two men who lived in Rome and were at different ends of the economic spectrum. Before gladiator contests in the Colesseum, everyone would stand, waiting silently for Caesar. The contests could not begin until he arrived. When he arrived, he was greeted with thunderous shouts of "Hail Caesar!" He had more power, prestige and wealth than anyone else living at that time. He was worshipped as though he were a god.

Elsewhere in Rome was another man in vastly different circumstances. He was in prison, chained to guards. He invested his time praying and writing to his friends. His name was Paul. One man lived in an opulent palace, the other in a dingy cell. One had almost unlimited wealth. The other had almost nothing. One was the centre of attention, the other was virtually ignored. Almost 2,000 years later, people around the world recognise which of these two men made the eternally important contribution. They name their children after the prisoner and their salads after the emperor! Being used by Christ in a significant way has nothing to do with a high position or great riches. It has everything to do with a willingness to allow Christ to become your Lord.

DO NOT BE CONFORMED TO THIS WORLD

Romans 12:2 begins with this command: "Do not conform any longer to the pattern of this world, but be transformed by the renewing of your mind. Then you will be able to test and approve what God's will is – his good, pleasing and perfect will."

We live in one of the most affluent cultures the world has ever known. And we are constantly bombarded with costly, manipulative advertising the purpose of which is to encourage us to spend money. Advertisers usually stress the importance of image rather than function. For example, car advertisements rarely focus on a car as reliable transportation that is economical to operate; instead, an image of status or sex appeal is projected.

Reflect on the claims of TV commercials. No matter what the product – clothing, deodorants, credit cards, cars, you name it – the message is communicated that the 'fulfilling, beautiful, wrinkle-free life' can be ours if we are willing to buy it. Unfortunately, this media onslaught has influenced all of us to some extent. One commentator put it this way "people buy things they do not need with money they do not have to impress people they do not even like."

The following graph depicts how the artificial, media-generated lifestyle influences our lives. The bottom curve represents our income – what we really can afford to buy. The next curve illustrates how much we actually spend. We make up the difference between our income and spending by the use of debt, which creates slavery, financial pressure and anxiety. The top of the graph demonstrates what advertisers tell us to buy. It is an image-conscious, generally expensive lifestyle that claims to satisfy the human heart's deepest needs. When we want to live this counterfeit, media-induced dream but cannot afford it, we suffer discontentment, envy and coveting.

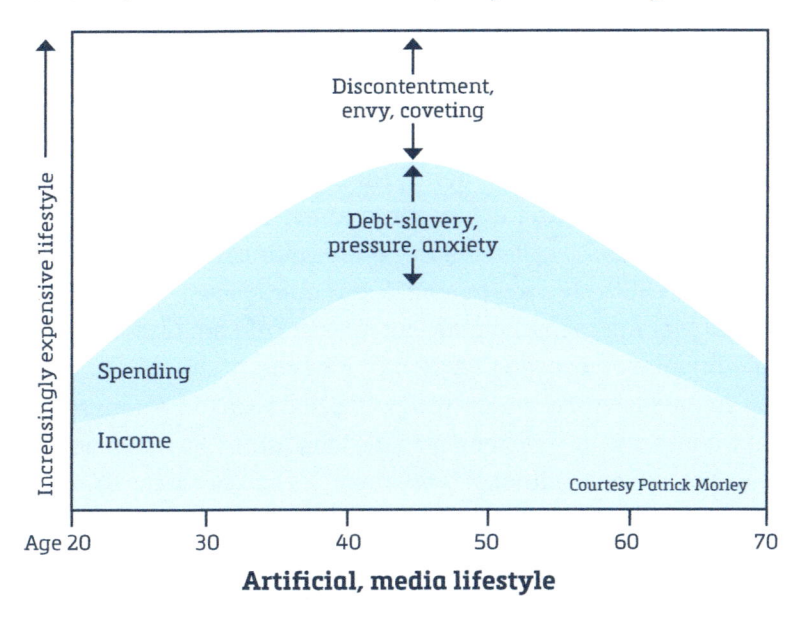

Artificial, media lifestyle

Courtesy Patrick Morley

None of us is immune to the lure of this message. Having completed our family spending plans for the year and decided not to go abroad, I recently found myself looking at a Sunday newspaper travel supplement advertising a wide range of cruising holidays. Every advert seemed to have discounted cruises to every conceivable destination. My wife had always wanted to go to the Norwegian fjords, while I had talked about a cruise in Eastern Europe. I was hooked! Then reality took over. Even after the discounts the cost was going to be several thousand pounds. How did that compare to our international travel budget of £nil? About ten minutes after opening the supplement, I jettisoned it onto the pile of other supplements and returned to the sports pages.

Shortly afterwards I received a letter from the manufacturer of my car advising me that I was due to pay £900 for my next year's warranty. I hadn't even thought about including this in my spending plan. I was in something resembling a state of shock. I contemplated the fact that the car was due for a service and calculated that this was going to cost me about £1,500. As I drove past the garage I saw a newer model. Instead of 35,000 miles on the clock, this one had only 8,000. For this used car I was only going to have to pay an additional £5,000. We did as we always do in situations like this: we thanked the salesman for his help and returned home. The next day I saw an advert in the newspaper, with the following words: 'Warranty expired or about to expire?' I called the free phone number and received a quote of £500. With a repair bill less than expected, I was only £400 over my spending plan, but at least I did not respond to my impulse and spend £5,000 on a new car.

In the space of a week my impulses had been to treat myself to a cruise and to 'save money in the long run' by buying a new car. Not following either of these impulses had saved me £7,500! What is more I had lost the desire for both the new car and the cruise. Interestingly enough, with half a day spent cleaning the car inside and out it looks and feels just like a new one!

Did prayer figure in all of this? Yes. Why would I do anything without referring to God. He is, after all, the owner, and I am the steward.

From time to time we all get hooked on something we think we must buy – a car, smartphone, camera, holiday, clothes, you name it. Once hooked, it is easy to rationalise a purchase. Please remember to seek the Lord's guidance and the counsel of a godly person when confronted with an impulse spending decision.

"Do not conform any longer to the pattern of this world, but be transformed by the renewing of your mind. Then you will be able to test and approve what God's will is – his good, pleasing and perfect will."

Romans 12:2

Perspectives

Turn on the television news and it will not be long before you hear of an event that has changed someone's life forever. It might be a coach crash, a weather disaster, a murder and so on. You may recall the flames that engulfed Matilda, Claudia Winkleman's daughter, at a Halloween party. One minute the young girl and mother are enjoying the party, the next... .

Money problems can also cause massive changes in people – the things they do, the way they respond, their happiness. Remember the John Cleese divorce tour? Cleese told everyone that he was only going back on the road to pay for his divorce. 'Lack of [enough] money', caused him to do something he really did not wish to do.

Money problems can cause people to become depressed. Money problems can even cause people to be suicidal, as we saw in the aftermath of the 2008 global financial crisis.

Money problems can be life-changing, and that is why the Lord sets out His financial plan for us to follow.

The futility of riches is stated very plainly in two places: the Bible and the tax return form.

What a Christian needs in the area of the handling of money and possessions is a biblical perspective.

MONEY WILL NOT BRING TRUE HAPPINESS

Solomon, the author of Ecclesiastes, had an annual income of more than £15 million. He lived in a palace that took 13 years to build. He owned 40,000 stalls of horses. He sat on an ivory throne overlaid with gold. He drank from gold cups. The daily menu of his household included one hundred sheep and thirty oxen in addition to fallow deer and fatted fowl. Obviously, Solomon was in a position to know whether money would bring happiness, and he did not hesitate to say that riches do not bring true happiness: "He who loves money shall never have enough. The foolishness of thinking that wealth brings happiness! The more you have, the more you spend, right up to the limits of your income" (Ecclesiastes 5:10–11, TLB).

In contrast, most people believe you can buy happiness.

"If only I had a new car, I would be satisfied". "If only I lived in that nice house, I would be content". "If only I had a particular job, I would be happy". The list is endless.

The Bible offers a sharp contrast to this attitude. As someone has said,

Money will buy:

- A bed but not sleep;
- Books but not brains;
- Food but not an appetite;
- A house but not a home;
- Medicine but not health;
- Amusement but not happiness;
- A crucifix but not a Saviour.

IS MONEY EVIL?

Money is not intrinsically evil. It is morally neutral. Money can be used for good, such as supporting missionaries or building hospitals. It also can be used for evil, such as financing illegal drugs and pornography.

Examine 1 Timothy 6:10 carefully: "The love of money is a root of all kinds of evil." The Bible does not condemn money itself, only the misuse of or a wrong attitude toward money. Moreover, particularly in the Old Testament, many of the godliest people were among the wealthiest people of the day. Job, Abraham and David were all wealthy, and yet they did not allow wealth to interfere with their relationship with the Lord.

Nevertheless, Scripture warns that riches can destroy a spiritually fruitful life! "The one who received the seed that fell among the thorns is the man who hears the word, but the worries of this life and the deceitfulness of wealth choke it, making it unfruitful" (Matthew 13:22).

Also, it is easy for those who are rich to turn away from God. "When I have brought them into the land flowing with milk and honey, the land I promised on oath to their forefathers, and when they eat their fill and thrive, they will turn to other gods and worship them, rejecting me and breaking my covenant" (Deuteronomy 31:20). Someone once observed "For every 99 people who can be poor and remain close to Christ, only one can become wealthy and maintain close fellowship with Him." It must be human nature to cling to the Lord when it's obvious that only He can provide our needs. Once people become wealthy, they often take the Lord for granted because they no longer think they have as much need of Him. "Those who love money will never have enough. How meaningless to think that wealth brings true happiness!" Ecclesiastes 5:10, NLT

WILL GODLY PEOPLE ALWAYS PROSPER FINANCIALLY?

Some Christians embrace one of two extremes. Some say if you are really spiritual, you must be poor because wealth and a close relationship with Christ cannot coexist. The second and opposite extreme is the belief that if a Christian has faith, he or she will enjoy uninterrupted financial prosperity.

One end of the spectrum teaches that godliness can occur only in an environment of poverty. However, we have already have noted that money is morally neutral and can be used for good or evil. In the Old Testament the Lord extended the reward of abundance to the people of Israel when they were obedient, while the threat of poverty was one of the consequences of disobedience. Deuteronomy 30:15-16 reads "I set before you today life and prosperity, death and destruction. For I command you today to love the Lord your God, to walk in his ways, and to keep his commands...and the Lord your God will bless you in the land you are entering to possess."

Moreover, Psalm 35:27 reads "let the Lord be magnified, who has pleasure in the prosperity of His servant." We may also pray for prosperity when our relationship with the Lord is healthy: "Beloved, I pray that you may prosper in all things and be in health, just as your soul prospers" (3 John 2, NKJV). The Bible does not say that a godly person must live in poverty. A godly person may have material resources.

There are those who believe all Christians who truly have faith will always prosper. This extreme also is in error.

Study the life of Joseph. He is the classic example of a faithful person who experienced both prosperity and poverty. He was born into a prosperous family, then was thrown into a pit and sold into slavery by his jealous brothers. He became a household slave in a wealthy Egyptian's home. His master, Potiphar, promoted Joseph to head the household. Later, Joseph made the righteous decision not to commit adultery with Potiphar's wife. Because of that decision, however, he was thrown into prison for years. In God's timing Joseph ultimately was elevated to the position of prime minister of Egypt.

LET'S EXAMINE FOUR REASONS WHY THE GODLY MAY NOT PROSPER:

1. VIOLATING A SCRIPTURAL PRINCIPLE

You may be giving generously but acting dishonestly. You may be honest but not properly fulfilling your work responsibilities. You may be a faithful employee but head-over-heels in debt. You may be completely out of debt but not giving.

One of the biggest benefits of **Bought** is that we explore what the entire Bible teaches about money. Those who do not understand all the requirements may neglect critical areas of responsibility. If they suffer financially, they may be confused about the reason for their lack of prosperity.

2. BUILDING GODLY CHARACTER

Romans 5:3-4, (NLT) reads "we can rejoice, too, when we run into problems and trials, for we know that they help us develop endurance. And endurance develops strength of character, and character strengthens our confident hope of salvation." An example of the Lord developing character in a people before prospering them is found in Deuteronomy 8:16-18: "He fed you with manna in the wilderness, a food unknown to your ancestors. He did this to humble you and test you for your own good. He did all this so you would never say to yourself, 'I have achieved this wealth with my own strength and energy.' Remember the Lord your God. He is the one who gives you power to be successful, in order to fulfil the covenant he confirmed to your ancestors with an oath."

The Lord knew the people of Israel had to be humbled before they could handle wealth. Our Father knows us better than we know ourselves. In His infinite wisdom He knows exactly how much He can entrust to us at any time without harming our relationship with Him.

3. THE MYSTERY OF GOD'S SOVEREIGNTY

Hebrews 11:1–35 lists people who triumphed miraculously by exercising their faith in the living God. But in verse 36 the writer directs our attention abruptly to godly people who lived by faith and gained God's approval, yet experienced poverty. The Lord ultimately chooses how much to entrust to each person. And sometimes we simply can't understand or explain His decisions.

Let's summarise thus far: the Scriptures teach neither the necessity of poverty nor uninterrupted prosperity. What the Bible teaches is the responsibility of being a faithful steward. Please review the following chart and the contrasts between the three perspectives.

	Poverty	Stewardship	Prosperity
Possessions are:	Evil	A responsibility	A right
I work to:	Meet only basic needs	Serve Christ	Become rich
Godly people are:	Poor	Faithful	Wealthy
Ungodly people are:	Wealthy	Unfaithful	Poor
I give:	Because I must	Because I love God	To get
My spending is:	Without gratitude to God	Prayerful and responsible	Carefree and consumptive

4. THE RICH EXPLOIT THE POOR

A fourth reason why the godly may not prosper is that they are exploited and oppressed, not paid a living wage. Amos 2:6-7 tells us "This is what the Lord says: 'For three sins of Israel, even for four, I will not turn back my wrath. They sell the righteous for silver and the needy for a pair of sandals. They trample on the heads of the poor as upon the dust of the ground and deny justice to the oppressed.'" The prophets repeatedly warn Israel against practising injustice and hurting the poor.

THE LORD'S PERSPECTIVE ON PROSPERITY

Before we leave the issue of prosperity, it is important to understand the Lord's perspective of prosperity is contrary to that of our culture. The Lord evaluates true riches based on His spiritual value system. This contrast is stated most clearly in the book of Revelation. The godly poor are rich in God's sight. "I [the Lord] know your tribulation and your poverty (but you are rich)" (Revelation 2:9). Those who are wealthy yet do not enjoy a close relationship with Christ are actually poor. "You say, 'I am rich; I have acquired wealth and do not need a thing.' But you do not realise that you are wretched, pitiful, poor, blind and naked" (Revelation 3:17). True prosperity extends far beyond material possessions. True prosperity is gauged by how well we know Jesus Christ and by how closely we follow Him.

INSTRUCTIONS TO THOSE WHO ARE RICH

Are you rich? Sometimes I feel rich and sometimes I don't. It usually depends on who I am around. Most of us define a rich person as someone who has more money than we do. But if we compare our living standards to all the people who have lived throughout history, or even with the rest of the billions of people living on the earth today, the majority of us who live in the UK are rich.

The Lord knew the rich would face serious spiritual danger. So Scripture offers three instructions for "those who are rich in this present world" (1 Timothy 6:17).

1. DO NOT BE CONCEITED

"Command those who are rich in this present world not to be arrogant" (1 Timothy 6:17).

What is your attitude toward those who beg or sell copies of the Big Issue? I recall on one occasion listening to a pastor from Reading who one Sunday morning disguised himself as a tramp and sat on the pavement about 100 metres down the road from the church. He sat watching with his collecting bowl as his church members walked past. Some ignored him. Some dropped a few pennies into his box. He watched others crossing the road only to cross back to walk into church. With ten minutes of the service elapsed, he picked himself up, ran round to the church's back entrance, changed and took his seat and joined in the singing. It was his turn to preach that day. Can you imagine the surprise and embarrassment when he asked the congregation who had seen the tramp and crossed to the other side of the road? Imagine their sense of guilt when he revealed that it was their preacher and pastor dressed in old and tatty attire.

James 1:9-10 addresses this issue: "The brother in humble circumstances ought to take pride in his high position. But the one who is rich should take pride in his low position, because he will pass away like a wild flower."

The poor should be encouraged as children of the King of kings, while the rich are to remain humble because life is short. If you are rich, you need the constant reminder to be humble before the Lord and other people.

2. PUT NO CONFIDENCE IN YOUR ASSETS

"Command those who are rich in this present world not to be arrogant nor to put their hope in wealth, which is so uncertain, but to put their hope in God, who richly provides us with everything for our enjoyment" (1 Timothy 6:17). For those who have riches, this is unlikely to be easy. In fact this may well present something of a struggle. When I first started studying biblical finance, I began to understand more fully the verses regarding God's ownership. Bit by bit, the pieces of my financial jigsaw started to fit together. I had accumulated wealth partly by not drawing any income from my businesses other than a basic minimum salary. Then I started to realise that I had been storing up finance because God had a plan to engage me to work in the stewardship ministry. I hadn't consciously said to the Lord "I know it all belongs to you", but neither had I ever regarded it as mine to spend. Did I get everything right according to Scripture? No. I was over 30 before I recognised the need to tithe. Have I always given? Yes. But have I always given generously? No. Have I put my trust in my assets? Yes. Do I put my trust in assets today? Nowhere near as much as I used to. I recently said to Rhoda, "Well, I came into this world with nothing, and I am prepared to end up with nothing. I am only ever one step from eternity, and I do not want my days here to be anything other than full of obedience to God."

It is easy to trust in money, for money can buy goods and services. It has so much power that it is easy to be fooled into thinking that money supplies our needs and offers security. Money can become our first love. We tend to trust in the seen rather than in the invisible, living God. This is why we need to remind ourselves to walk by faith rather than by sight.

3. GIVE GENEROUSLY

"Command them to do good, to be rich in good deeds, and to be generous and willing to share. In this way they will lay up treasure for themselves as a firm foundation for the coming age, so that they may take hold of the life that is truly life" (1 Timothy 6:18-19).

As I suggested before, one of the most effective antidotes for the potential disease of loving money is 'setting the finish line'. Determine a maximum amount that you will accumulate. After you have reached your goal, give the rest to build God's kingdom.

HOW MUCH IS ENOUGH?

This is a question that is often asked.

I sold my last business when I was 49 and purposed in my

heart that increasing my wealth was not even on my agenda. Did I have 'enough'? Well, I thought I did and then the stock market collapsed and interest rates hit the floor. But I had made my decision and rested at peace.

Subsequently, the Lord gave me the ability to earn income from contracting to write for one of the companies I had founded, and also lecturing professionals on the art of professional firm management. In so doing I have been able to use part of this revenue to live and part to invest in the Lord's work. Would I like to have more? The question rarely enters into my thinking, and when it does I dismiss it immediately.

Oh, and the answer to the question for many? – when is enough enough? When I have just a little bit more!

How much is enough?
For many, the answer to that question is
'When I have a little more.'

Consider this

Save. Invest. Spend.

GET MORE INSIGHTS AT
→ WWW.YOURMONEYCOUNTS.ORG.UK

Wise stewards save for the future.

Resist the temptation to indulge in any form of gambling, gaming or lottery activities.

Build a short term savings fund to cover emergencies.

Set your finances in order with a balanced spending plan that embraces all that you feel you have learned and wish to apply from this book.

Check the balances on your financial accounts regularly.

Key Questions

Do you have a saving and investment plan?

Do you have immediate access to adequate short term savings?

Are your investments diversified?

Do you have a balanced spending plan?

Could you live more simply?

6

Summing it all up

Do you feel like you are in a crisis?

I have endeavoured to cover as many of the major biblical financial principles as the pages of **Bought** allow. The Bible is truly a book that speaks right into today's culture directly into the challenges that so many face. Timothy tells us that all Scripture is profitable for teaching – how wonderful that we have this 'handbook' to lead and guide us with how we handle our money and possessions.

PART 6 | CHAPTER 15

Do you feel like you are in a crisis?

The official motto of the United States is "In God we trust." Trusting Him at all times is central to the life of a Christian. This journey of trust and relationship with God Himself will be a tower of power in a crisis. Many have lost a job or become long term sick, and their income stream has suddenly reduced. Trusting God and being wise in the good times is evidence of the life of the wise steward.

Do you feel you are in a financial crisis? Maybe you have read this book and finally see that there is but one final part and two more chapters to go. You have diligently studied the book and sought to apply Scripture to your situation.

I have known many people who have faced a financial crisis. In my days as an accountant I saw businessmen cry as they faced the reality of losing their home as a consequence of a failed business, and a bank seeking their pound of flesh; women whose husbands had abandoned them – in one case a lady with five children whose husband completely disappeared, leaving her with nothing other than debts of over £100,000 and minimal income. I asked her how close she was to jumping off the Clifton Suspension Bridge. She broke down crying. She was beyond being desperate.

I have known a number of situations where one spouse had debts the other did not know about. If that is you – then it is time to open up, repent and walk through the journey of addressing the problem – which is likely to be more than just financial. Deal with this now, before the problem becomes even greater. I know of one family where the breadwinner became terminally ill and had no income other than state welfare. I have known students worry about their debt and leave their course because they could not handle the financial pressure. There were people who have so much inherited wealth they did not work and led a life of little purpose or value.

And I am sure you can think of others who face, other than maybe yourself, who face a crisis.

Some challenges build slowly and can be anticipated; others appear without warning. Some are resolved quickly; others are chronic. Some reflect the consequences of our actions; others are completely beyond our control. Some crises impact an entire nation; others are isolated to individuals.

A job loss, major illness, birth of a special-needs child, business reversal, death of a family member, identity theft, military deployment of a breadwinner, withdrawal or reduction in state benefits, home repossession, bankruptcy or a worldwide financial crisis are examples of situations that can exert major pressure on a household and its finances. Surveys reveal that many marriages struggle and sometimes don't survive the stress of these difficulties.

These challenges can be seen as the 'storms of life'. But while some of the storms amount to little more than a blustery rain shower, others feel like a category five hurricane.

Please remember this one thing: no matter what the crisis, you don't face it alone. Jesus Christ is with you every step of the way.

Put yourself in the sandals of a few of God's people in the Bible who faced terrifying storms:

- Job—in a matter of just a few hours—lost his children, his financial resources, and ultimately his health.

- Joseph was sold into slavery and thrown into prison.
- Moses and the Israelites faced annihilation by Egypt's powerful army at the Red Sea.
- Daniel was tossed into the lions' den.
- Paul was beaten, stoned and left for dead on his missionary journeys.

The list goes on and on.

Although storms are often emotional, scary and painful, if we maintain God's perspective, we can survive and even grow through such dark days and nights!

GOD'S ROLE

When facing a crisis, nothing is more important than knowing who God is—His love, care, guidance, control and power. Only the Bible reveals the true extent of God's involvement in our challenges. If we have an inadequate or warped view of God and His purposes, then we won't fully embrace and learn from our challenges. What's more, we will forfeit the peace, contentment and even joy that God makes available to us in the midst of the storm.

GOD LOVES YOU

Firstly, John 4:8 sums up God's very nature: God is love. God loves you, and throughout your whole life remains intimately involved with you as an individual. Psalm 139:17 reveals, "How precious are your thoughts concerning me, O God! How vast is the sum of them! Were I to count them, they would outnumber the grains of sand." In other words, the Creator of the universe is always thinking about you!

When you think about it, John 15:9 has to be one of the most encouraging verses in all of the Bible. Jesus says to His disciples: "As the Father has loved me, so I have loved you". Don't read these words lightly! Allow the implications to sink in for a moment. Consider how much God the Father loves God the Son. They have existed forever in the closest possible relationship with a deep, unfathomable love for each other. And Jesus says this is how much He loves you!

In any crisis, it's critical to be reminded of God's unfailing love and faithfulness. Why? Because it's so very easy to become discouraged and even lose hope in such times. It's easy to forget God's love and care for you, especially when adversity first strikes—or goes on and on for what feels like an eternity.

Jeremiah the prophet was completely discouraged. He wrote: "I remember my affliction and my wandering, the bitterness...and my soul is downcast within me" (Lamentations 3:19-20). But then he remembered the Lord "Yet I call this to mind and therefore have hope. Because of the Lord's great love we are not consumed, for his compassions never fail. They are new every morning; great is your faithfulness" (Lamentations 3:21-23).

It is helpful to meditate on passages such as these: God has said "Never will I leave you; never will I forsake you.' So we can say with confidence, 'The Lord is my helper; I will not be afraid. What can man do to me?'" (Hebrews 13:5-6). "Who shall separate us from the love of Christ? Shall trouble or hardship or persecution or famine or nakedness or danger or sword? .... No, in all these things we are more than conquerors through him who loved us" (Romans 8:35, 37).

Even in a crisis, the Lord will do kind things that offer clear evidence of His love and care for us. Consider Joseph. While a slave, [Joseph's] "master saw that the Lord was with him" (Genesis 39:3), so his master put him in charge of all he owned. Later, in prison, "the Lord was with Joseph and extended kindness to him, and gave him favour in the sight of the chief jailer" (Genesis 39:21).

GOD IS IN CONTROL

God is ultimately in control of every event. This is but a sampling of passages that affirm His control: "Our God is in the heavens; He does whatever He pleases" (Psalm 115:3). "We adore you as being in control of everything" (1 Chronicles 29:11, TLB). "Whatever the Lord pleases, He does, in heaven and in earth" (Psalm 135:6). "My [the Lord's] purpose will stand, and I will do all that I please" (Isaiah 46:10, NIV). "For nothing will be impossible with God" (Luke 1:37).

The Lord is in control even of difficult events. "I am the Lord, and there is no other, The One forming light and creating darkness, causing well-being and creating calamity; I am the Lord who does all these" (Isaiah 45:6-7).

GOD HAS A PURPOSE IN ADVERSITY

The Cecropia moth emerges from its cocoon only after a long, exhausting struggle to free itself. A young boy, wishing to help the moth, carefully slit the exterior of the cocoon. Soon it came out, but its wings were shrivelled and couldn't function. What the young boy didn't realise was that the moth's struggle to liberate itself from the cocoon was essential to develop its wings—and its ability to fly.

Much like the cocoon of the Cecropia moth, adversity has a part to play in our lives as well. God uses those difficult, sometimes heart-breaking times to mature us in Christ. James 1:2-4 says it this way: "Consider it pure joy, my brothers, whenever you face trials of many kinds, because you know that the testing of your faith develops perseverance. Perseverance must finish its work so that you may be mature and complete, not lacking anything".

God uses and sometimes designs challenging circumstances for our ultimate benefit. Romans 8:28-29 tells us "We know that in all things God works for the good of those who love Him, who have been called according to His purpose. For those God foreknew he also predestined to be conformed to the likeness of his Son..." And the primary good that God works in our lives is to make us more like Christ.

We see this same thought expressed in Hebrews 12:6, 10-11 "For those whom the Lord loves He disciplines.... God disciplines us for our good that we may share in his holiness. All discipline for the moment seems not to be joyful but sorrowful; yet to those who have been trained by it, afterwards it yields the peaceful fruit of righteousness." God makes no mistakes. He knows exactly what He wants us to become and also knows exactly what is necessary to produce that result in our lives.

Evangelist Alan Redpath captures this truth: "There is nothing—no circumstances, no trouble, no testing—that can ever touch me until, first of all, it has gone past God, past Christ, right through to me. If it has come that far, it has come with great purpose, which I may not understand at the moment. But as I refuse to become panicky, as I lift my eyes to Him and accept it as coming from the throne of God for some great purpose of blessing to my own heart, no sorrow will ever disturb me, no trial will ever disarm me, no circumstance will cause me to fret, for I shall rest in the joy of what my Lord is."

You can be comforted knowing that your loving heavenly Father is in absolute control of every situation you will ever face. He intends to use each circumstance for a good purpose. 1 Thessalonians 5:18 says it well: "Give thanks in all circumstances, for this is God's will for you in Christ Jesus."

TRUSTING GOD

We should view crises through the lens of God's love, faithfulness and control.

The Bible makes it clear that God offers security only in Himself—not in money, not in possessions, not in a career, and not in other people. External things offer the illusion of security, but the Lord alone can be fully trusted. "The Lord is good, a refuge in times of trouble. He cares for those who trust in Him" (Nahum 1:7, NIV). "When I am afraid, I will trust in you. In God, whose word I praise, in God I trust; I will not be afraid" (Psalm 56:3-4).

THE EYE OF THE STORM

There are several things we can do to survive—and even grow—when we find ourselves in the storm. Recognise difficulties as opportunities to grow into the people God wants us to be. In adversity we learn things we just couldn't learn any other way.

Yes, that is easy to say and I realise I cannot possibly know your circumstances. But, trusting in the Lord in the tough times is an acid test of your faith. When the going gets tough, the tough get going. Remember that you are accompanied by the full armour of God.

GET YOUR FINANCIAL HOUSE IN ORDER

I've known many people with financial problems – all of them looking to overcome their problem. "What can I do?" they ask.

Jesus answers the question this way in Matthew 7:24-25: "Everyone who hears these words of mine and puts them into practice is like a wise man who built his house on the rock. The rain came down, the streams rose, and the winds blew and beat against that house; yet it did not fall, because it had its foundation on the rock."

The key to solving your financial problems is learning and applying God's way of handling money. It truly is that simple. That's why what we have shared in this book is so important. You have nearly finished the book and so have a much greater grasp of God's framework for managing money. But knowing is only half of what you need. The other half is applying what you have learned. It may take a long time and a lot of effort to apply these principles or to navigate the storm, but you will know the basics of what you should do.

Part of what you've learned is to be a generous giver. When facing a financial crisis the tendency is to hold on tightly to what we have, and become less generous. A key passage in the book of Acts, however, shows us a different way. In Acts 11:28-29, we read: "Agabus [a prophet]...through the Spirit predicted that a severe famine would spread over the entire Roman world. (This happened during the reign of Claudius.) The disciples, each according to his ability, decided to provide help for the brothers living in Judea".

The Holy Spirit revealed through a prophet that a severe famine was coming soon, and their first reaction was to get out their money! Don't allow a crisis or a pending crisis to stop you from remaining generous. You may not be able to give as much as you did previously, but still give.

It's also important to evaluate quickly how the circumstance will impact your finances, and to make the necessary adjustments for any diminished income or increased expenses. And don't forget to communicate! Tell the Lord, and if you are married, tell each other your feelings and concerns. How important is this? It's important enough to schedule a time every day to share, so you can encourage each other. Rhoda and I discovered that a crisis doesn't have to damage our marriage; in fact, it can be a catalyst to improve it. I am fully persuaded that God intends married couples to grow closer together during a crisis rather than allowing the difficulties to damage their marriage. Never go through a storm alone. As already mentioned, it is important not to go it alone. It is almost impossible to make the wisest decisions in isolation when experiencing a crisis. Seek advice from people who have been through similar situations. You will draw strength not only from their emotional support, but also from their experience. There are people all around you who have weathered serious life storms, and you can gain from their knowledge, learning about mistakes to avoid and of resources to help. Ask your church and friends to pray; it's their most powerful contribution.

LIVE ONE DAY AT A TIME

Live focused on today as well as with an eye on tomorrow – even though you do not know what the day may bring. And if the crisis becomes severe, focus on one moment at a time in close fellowship with Christ. This is not 'escape from reality', but rather, it is a practical way to stay close to the only One who can help you through the challenge.

BE PATIENT, WAITING FOR GOD'S TIMING

Expectations can be damaging during a crisis. When we assume that the Lord will solve our problems in a certain way by a certain time, we set ourselves up for disappointment and frustration.

Someone once described patience as accepting a difficult situation without giving God a deadline for removing it. Remember, God's primary purpose in allowing a crisis in the first place is to conform you to Jesus Christ. He is at work in your life and knows exactly how long it will take to produce the results He wants. Ecclesiastes 3:1 says "There is an appointed time for everything. And there is a time for every event under heaven."

You may smile when I say that "God is seldom early, but He's never late." Remember Sarah and Abraham? Genesis 18: 13-14 tells us: "When the Lord said to Abraham "Why did Sarah laugh? Why did she say, 'Can an old woman like me have a baby?' Is anything too hard for the Lord? I will return about this time next year, and Sarah will have a son." Sarah was 91 before she gave birth. But Romans 4: 19-21 tells us that, "Without weakening in his faith, he faced the fact that his body was as good as dead—since he was about a hundred years old—and that Sarah's womb was also dead. Yet he did not waver through unbelief regarding the promise of God, but was strengthened in his faith and gave glory to God, being fully persuaded that God had power to do what he had promised."

Trust the Lord your God. Seek His guidance – prayer and the Bible are a good starting point. Be patient. Be careful not to set deadlines for the Lord to act.

Work diligently to solve your problems, with the recognition that you need the moment-by-moment help and counsel of the Lord who loves you. Philippians 4:6-7 is one of those Bible passages that comes 'fully loaded' and is very helpful for those facing a crisis. "Be anxious for nothing but in everything by prayer and supplication with thanksgiving let your request be made known to God and the peace of God which surpasses all understanding will guard your heart and mind in Christ Jesus."

FORGIVE OTHERS

Imagine you are a teenager, deeply loved by your father. Your siblings sell you into slavery, and for the next 13 years you are a slave and a prisoner. Amazingly, on one unbelievable day, you find yourself elevated to second in command of the world's most powerful nation. Several years later, your starving siblings—the ones who betrayed you—beg you for food. What's your response: retaliation or forgiveness?

This is the question Joseph had to answer, and he forgave. How was he able to do this? Because he recognised that God had orchestrated his circumstances—even the ones that were so deeply traumatic and painful. "God sent me ahead of you... he told his brothers, to save your lives by a great deliverance. So then, it was not you who sent me here, but God" (Genesis 45:7-8, NIV).

God realises how critical it is for us to forgive those who are involved in causing our crisis, regardless of their motivation. One of the most impressive characteristics of Jesus Christ was His willingness to forgive. Imagine hanging on a cross in excruciating agony, and at the same time praying for those who had crucified you: "Father, forgive them for they do not know what they are doing" (Luke 23:34).

When the apostle Peter asked Jesus if he should forgive

someone seven times, He responded, not seven times, but seventy-seven times" (Matthew 18:22). He then told a parable about a servant who was forgiven a large debt by his master but refused to forgive a fellow servant a small debt. Christ describes what happens to the unforgiving servant: "In anger his master turned him over to the jailers to be tortured until he should pay back all he owed. This is how my heavenly Father will treat each of you unless you forgive your brother from the heart" (Matthew 18:34-35).

In order to grow more like Christ and experience the benefits He intends for us during a crisis, we must forgive. And more than forgive, we are to be kind, compassionate, and seek to be a blessing. "Be kind and compassionate to one another, forgiving each other, just as in Christ, God forgave you" (Ephesians 4:32). "Not returning evil for evil, or insult for insult, but giving a blessing instead; for you were called for the very purpose that you might inherit a blessing" (1 Peter 3:9).

Unforgiveness can be a daily battle, particularly if the crisis has been horribly hurtful. But it harms the person who refuses to forgive.

It is imperative to pray regularly for the Lord to give us the desire to forgive, and then to give us His love for the people who may have harmed us. Jesus tells us also to pray for them, "Love your enemies and pray for those who persecute you, that you may be sons of your Father in heaven" (Matthew 5:44-45). It's hard to remain bitter toward someone for whom you are praying regularly.

COMMON CHALLENGES

Let's examine two of the most common financial challenges people face.

JOB LOSS

Losing your job ranks among one of life's most stressful events, especially if the loss is unexpected—not just for you, but for your spouse as well if you are married. Meet together as soon as possible after the news of the job loss, and discuss ways to minimise the emotional and financial toll on both of you. And encourage each other because often a job loss is a blessing in disguise. God may bring you a better career opportunity, and it can build your faith as you experience Him providing for your needs even without a job.

Next, formulate a game plan for the job search—from drafting a CV to networking with friends and searching online. When you lose a job, your full-time occupation should be finding a new job.

In addition to cutting back on spending for discretionary items, there are two financial goals to keep in mind. First, make every effort to avoid using debt to meet living expenses. Many people mask the real situation by using debt to fund current spending. Make good, hard decisions not to spend one penny you don't have to. Every borrowed penny must be repaid with interest, and although spending it is easy, repayment is always hard work.

Second, contact your creditors early before they start to send unwanted demands and threats. Most companies will look sympathetically at requests for payment deferrals or, alternatively, for reduced payments.

Thirdly, do all you can to maintain insurance payments. These may be for life assurance or perhaps sickness insurance.

ILLNESS OR ACCIDENT

If you suffer a major illness or accident, your normal income may reduce unless you have a good insurance policy, and additional costs will result. In fact, this situation, if going to impact long term, can be catastrophic. I have two church friends, Ian and Dave, who both had a life-changing accident on a motor cycle. They were both young when their accidents happened. While trusting the Lord and having a testimony concerning His love and healing power, they both discovered that they were no longer able to work again. Life changed in just one split second. Thankful? Yes, for their lives being spared.

If married, be prepared for the possibility that one of you may need to make important decisions without the benefit of input from the other.

Don't be embarrassed to make your needs known to your family, friends and church. Extend to them the opportunity to help meet your needs. Giving to those in need is a big part of what it means to follow Christ. Galatians 6:2 reminds us: "Carry each other's burdens, and in this way you will fulfil the law of Christ".

PREPARING FOR FUTURE STORMS

You can't prevent every difficulty, but you can prepare to survive them by building a solid relationship with the Lord—and your spouse, if you are married—and by improving your finances. The healthier your finances, the better you will be able to cope. Proverbs 27:12 says, "The prudent see danger and take refuge, but the simple keep going and suffer for it".

The more time you spend getting to know God and what He reveals in the Bible—and applying what you've learned—the better prepared you will be to weather life's storms.

Gerald Crabbe wrote "Through the Fire". I find the words of this song have such a deep meaning and understanding of life.

> "So many times I question the certain circumstances and things I could not understand.
> Many times in trials my weakness blurs my vision that's when my frustration seems gets so out of hand.
> It's then I am reminded, I've never been forsaken. I've never had to stand one test alone.
> That's when I look at all the victories, the Spirit rising up in me.
> And It's through the fire my weakness is made strong.
> He never promised that the cross would not get heavy and the hill would not be hard to climb.

> He never offered victories without fighting but He
> said help would always come in time.
> Just remember when you're standing in the valley
> of decision and the adversary says give in, Just hold
> on. Our Lord will show up (YES) and He will take you
> through the fire again
> I know within myself that I would surely perish
> If I trust the hand of God, He'll shield the flame again,
> again!"

Hear the full impact by listening to this online - enter Through The Fire into the You Tube search function.

At the beginning of **Bought** we asked why the Bible has 2,350 verses about money and possessions. The Lord knew that how we handled money would help determine the intimacy of our fellowship with Him. The Lord also wanted to provide us with a blueprint for handling money so that we could be faithful in this practical area of life.

> *There must be the conversion of the heart, the mind and also the purse.*

TAKE ACTION BUT GIVE YOURSELF TIME

The fundamental truth for us to understand is that God has retained the responsibilities of ownership of possessions, control of events and provision of needs. We are not designed to shoulder these responsibilities. However, as we have read, the Lord delegated certain important tasks to us as stewards.

Applying these financial principles is a journey that takes

time. You are just starting the journey as you finish this book, and your finances are probably not yet aligned with the thoughts and decisions you have made as you read through the pages. Please don't get anxious or frustrated. It takes the average person at least a year to apply most of these principles. Why not look at the other material available. Visit our website at www.yourmoneycounts.org for further insight and information.

FAITHFULNESS IN SMALL MATTERS IS IMPORTANT

Because of a lack of resources many people become frustrated by their inability to solve their financial problems. Remember, simply be faithful with what you have – whether it is little or much.

Some give up too soon. They abandon the goal of becoming debt free. They stop trying to increase their saving or giving. For them the task seems impossible. And it may be impossible without the Lord's help. Your job is to make a genuine effort, no matter how small it may appear. Then leave the results to God. I love what the Lord said to the prophet Zechariah: "Who despises the day of small things?" (Zechariah 4:10). Don't be discouraged. Be diligent. Be persistent. Be faithful in even the smallest matters.

A good friend once asked me what was the most valuable lesson I had learned from studying biblical finance. I have reflected on that question for some time now and think the most valuable thing for me is to know what it means for God to be the owner of everything, to know that finances are to be and can be approached in a godly manner and to recognise that the Bible holds the keys to understanding what we have to do to be godly in the area of the handling of money and possessions.

In Romans 12:2 Paul presented this problem and the solution: "Do not conform any longer to the pattern of this world, but be transformed by the renewing of your mind."

The only way for any of us to renew our minds is to commit continually to studying and applying Scripture.

The Bible has the answers to the financial problems of the sophistications of the twenty-first century. The eternal principles of Scripture are practical in any culture and in any century.

CONTENTMENT

At the beginning of this book I said that one of our objectives was that you would learn to be content. 1 Timothy 6:8 issues this challenging statement: "But if we have food and clothing, we will be content with that." Study this passage carefully. It declares that if you have food and covering (clothes and shelter), you should be content. Our culture has restated this verse to read something like this: "If you can afford the finest food to eat, wear the latest fashions, drive the latest upmarket car and live in a beautiful house in the nicest area of town, then you can be happy." Nothing could be further from the truth. There are three elements in learning to be content:

1. Know what God requires of a steward

2. Fulfil those requirements faithfully

3. Trust God to do His part

Once we understand God's will and we have been faithful in fulfilling our responsibilities as stewards, we can be content. Our loving, heavenly Father will entrust us with the possessions He knows will be best for us at any particular time – whether much or little.

Biblical contentment is not to be equated with laziness, complacency, social insensitivity or apathy. Because we serve the living and dynamic God, Christians should always be improving. Contentment does not exclude properly motivated ambition. We have already discovered that God wants us to work hard. I believe we should have a burning desire to be faithful stewards of the talents and possessions He has entrusted to us. Biblical contentment is an inner peace that accepts what God has chosen for our present vocation, station in life and financial state. Hebrews 13:5 emphasises this: "Keep your lives free from the love of money and be content with what you have", because God has said, 'never will I leave you; never will I forsake you.'"

SETTING THIS BOOK FREE

Some years ago I was listening to a radio programme in Australia. That day the host was talking to an author who was encouraging listeners to 'set their books free'. Intrigued by the concept, I listened to the proposal which was to find a shopping mall, a phone booth or some other public place and leave a book for someone else to read. Searching the internet, I soon discovered that this is not an unknown practice. I thought of my own bookshelf and decided that passing books on was a good investment to make in the lives of others. Our country has millions who have financial problems and so I encourage you to find someone you know who you think would benefit from reading this book.

Consider this

Summing it all up

GET MORE INSIGHTS AT
→ WWW.YOURMONEYCOUNTS.ORG.UK

God is there in the midst of all life's storms if we have a real relationship with Him.

God has a purpose in our adversities.

It is important to create a plan that will put your financial house in order.

Forgive everyone – hold nothing against anyone.

Always trust the hand of God as He will shield you from the flames over and over again.

Key questions

Do you have a written plan? If not – then now is a good time to start on it!

Have you asked God to forgive you for any past sins and mistakes?

Do you have a spending plan and are you keeping to it?

Do you seek guidance from God regarding your life?

Do you know others that you may be able to help with their finances?